THE CHRISTIAN FELLOWSHIP

THE
CHRISTIAN
FELLOWSHIP

by

NELS F. S. FERRÉ, Ph.D.

Abbot Professor of Christian Theology
Andover Newton Theological School

HARPER & BROTHERS PUBLISHERS
New York and London

THE CHRISTIAN FELLOWSHIP

april 1953

To my mother,
a living symbol of Christian fellowship

CONTENTS

PREFACE

THE great challenge to-day to the Christian fellowship is the idea of the ecumenical church. Earnest Christians throughout the world and in all branches of Christendom are praying and working that the prayer of Christ that they all be one may come true. The greatest obstacle in the way is the fact that three approaches to Christianity seem irreconcilable. These are the literalistic, the liberal, and the sacramentarian. Honest Christians cannot become one by the forsaking of what they believe Christianity to be. They can come together only when they see so deeply into the nature of the Christian faith as to be inevitably united by it. This book is offered as an aid to that end. Its one and only theme is that deeper meaning of the Christian fellowship, which, when fully understood, can unite all Christendom.

The reader may be interested in learning how

the book came to be. At different times and by different groups, ranging from a laymen's group in Newton to the International Congregational Seminar on the Christian Church, the author was requested to prepare papers on various aspects of the Christian fellowship. These requests were strikingly united in theme, and all the problems represented could find solution only through a deeper understanding of the Christian fellowship.

An expression of gratitude for the courtesy of permitting the reprinting of material is due Harper and Brothers for Chapter III, enlarged and revised, from *Swedish Contributions to Modern Theology*, and to the *International Review of Missions* for Chapter VII.

The author wishes to thank his colleagues, Professor Emeritus Daniel Evans, Professor Amos N. Wilder, and Dr. Hugh Vernon White of Andover Newton Theological School, and Professor Edgar S. Brightman of Boston University for reading and criticizing certain parts of the manuscript. He is grateful also to his wife for her share in the preparation of the manuscript, and owes a great deal to his students who have struggled with him for a more adequate understanding of the pressing problems of Christian faith.

NELS F. S. FERRÉ

Newton Center, Mass.

THE CHRISTIAN FELLOWSHIP

sciousness may be, history provides a body of information concerning man's formal and informal experimentations and investigations which plays an important part in both individual and social action.

The purpose of this chapter is definitely not to investigate how the external world is known, nor to dispute concerning the philosophical consequences attendant upon the results of such an investigation; but, rather, to understand the social growth of knowledge and to inquire how knowledge can legitimately contribute to social and religious adequacy. The two foci of this study, therefore, ought to be validity, or demonstrable certainty, and adequacy, or social applicability. Our problem must consequently be how the two can be properly understood and meaningfully related.

If knowledge as a social act is to be correctly comprehended, the philosophic field must not be initially limited to some artificial abstraction, whether in idealistic or in realistic terms. Man's historic experience as a whole constitutes the social source of knowledge. The genetic fallacy, moreover, dooms equally the individualistic and the social approach. To explain how knowledge grows as a social process is to explain fully neither knowledge nor the nature of reality, but such an explanation may suggest standards and limits of what Dewey calls "warranted assertibility." It may at the same time reveal the limits of inadequate theories of knowledge. For our present purposes the philosophic field may be considered "the convergent and cumulative effect of continued inquiry that defines knowledge in its general meaning";[2] but for the very reason that the aim of this study is to understand the nature not only of validity, but also of adequacy, the philosophic method will not be restricted to scientific inquiry in any narrowing sense. Our method, rather, consists of the analysis, insofar as it is available for interpretation, of the fullness of man's historic experience. This approach may, therefore, be thought of as "synoptic analysis" or "analytical realism."

Analytical realism is not deductive in the sense that it assumes as ultimately true certain prin-

[2] Dewey, *Logic, The Theory of Inquiry*, p. 8.

ciples, however derived, building up from these by the principle of coherence an entire metaphysical system. Such deduction is not only abstractive, in common with all interpretation, but runs the danger of being disproportionately and only distantly related to experience as a whole. Nor is this analysis inductive in the sense that it begins with individual facts and by productive imagination or by creative will arrives at conclusions which subsequently explain these facts. The proper limit of inductive efficacy seems to be the establishing of the correct relation between a particular set of facts and a relevantly limited form. This relation may then include the discovery, the correction, or the extension of form. Experience as a whole, however, seems beyond the grasp of individual inductive interpretation. In terms of knowledge as a social act, of course, the method of analytical realism is thoroughly inductive, proceeding throughout from the facts of experience to the forms which can be gradually established as correctly related to it and then used abstractly in the pursuit of further knowledge. But this method depends more and more

upon the increasing capacity for and use of deductive processes. The gradual social growth of
inductively established and deductively usable
forms sets the stage for our present study.

At this point, however, the crux of the problem concerning knowledge as a social act becomes increasingly clear. Deductive reasoning is
most valid in the realm of pure form, whereas
inductive reasoning is most valid in the case of
scientifically controllable fact. Validity seems at
its maximum with the maximum of abstraction,
and at its minimum with the maximum of social
applicability. Demonstrability and objective
communicability approach absolute certainty at
the two opposite extremes of pure form and controllable fact, but diminish in proportion to the
loss of the purity of form and scientific observa-
bility characteristic of that fullness of life out of
which are fashioned conflicting social and religious interpretations. The logician dealing with
pure forms has a right to point to the mere prob-
ability, if that, of the conclusions of those who
have to try to solve the practical problems of
life. The natural scientist who eschews general

theory as much as possible and confines his interest to specific measurements and the ascertaining of definite facts may well lift an eyebrow when the social scientist or the philosopher of religion ponders solutions of living problems. Validity and adequacy are, however, two different things, for neither the logician nor the scientist can by this method offer men guidance in the present conflict of social philosophies. In a day when philosophy can turn national and theology political, to the extent that the foundations of science in civilization may become undermined, it is high time that philosophy try to become adequate in its approach, not at the expense of validity, but at the mid-point of the two types of validity, characterizing factual and formal abstractions, in order to synthesize as far as possible the two concepts of validity and adequacy.

Validity is largely a matter of consistency of form, on the one hand, and of demonstrability of fact in relation to form, on the other; and thus in both cases is a matter of abstraction from the fullness of experience. The necessity for an immediate choice between the two, however, if and insofar as this is possible, should never blind us to their necessary and continuous interaction whenever knowledge is viewed as a social act. There is a large and definite deductive element in all social growth of knowledge. The forms of fact have been patiently studied and described by intricate systems of learning which no isolated human individual could possibly have developed by himself. Every discoverer of new knowledge uses the results of ages of past investigation. The cumulative forms of the past serve the present as deductive forms, that is, as reliable abstractions in the sense that their applicability to experience has been established and verified to the point where they need not be continuously tested before they can be used. Even though the foci of fact and form seem opposite, there is, nevertheless, between them a world of reality to which both apply. Our problem is how to extend the area of applicable interpretation beyond the realm of natural uniformity to the living meaningfulness of our social situation.

In order to approach a solution to this problem, it seems necessary first to study the functional relation of deduction and induction; then to ascertain how new knowledge can be legitimately added to what we already know; and finally to suggest what kind of abstractions from validly tested experience can most adequately guide social creativity. Induction, as we have seen, is the going from the particularity of facts to forms common to these facts, which forms can then be abstractly expressed and manipulated, while being, at the same time, truly representative of the facts; or, if the process for the sake of testing the form be reversed, induction is the testing of selected forms as to their limit of applicability to appropriate particularity. The consequent establishment of scientific laws which possess purity of formal validity to a degree where they can function as mathematical formulas in isolation from all empirical data constitutes the capacity of these laws for deductive applicability when relevantly and proportionately abstractive. Centuries of investigation have made particular symbols applicably available for scientific manipulation without the necessity of recurring empirical investigation. Induction presupposes the objective reality of significant unities within the experiential content which are accessible to knowledge in accordance with the proper rules of correct observation and discriminating analysis. Since deduction as a method of knowing, on the other hand, is directly dependent on experience for applicable effectiveness, it is as distinctly related to experience as the forms which have first been abstracted from it.

The validity obtained through induction is really deductive applicability provided by the correct analysis of a particular field of facts in relation to the forms in which they function. The continuous purity of these forms is invariably subject to their correction by the discovery of recalcitrant facts relevant to these forms but themselves not subsumable under them. The forms are ever subject to re-examination in the light of the fuller or more correctly analyzed experiential process. The field of deduction is primarily that of logical validity; the field of induction is primarily that of empirical applicability. But neither method is self-sufficient. Induction arrives at rules through facts only in the sense that all principles deductively applicable have been inductively established through the methodical analysis of a carefully observed phase of experience. Empirical reality inclusive of its functional regularities is the source and standard of induction. The abstractive consistency of these regularities within experience is the source and standard of deduction. Every new inductive operation depends, if it represents any stage of advanced knowledge, upon the cumulative growth of deductively usable forms. Naturally, there are also decided deductive elements in the case of individual experience having biological roots, such as habit, but these interesting questions fall outside the scope and specific purpose of this investigation. There are, in any case, deductive elements in all knowledge without which knowledge is impossible. Analytical realism, therefore, aims at an interpretative synthesis of induction and deduction by resolute reference to the primary source of both. The functional forcefulness of deduction is increased in direct proportion to the degree of abstraction into the purity of form; the functional forcefulness of induction is increased in direct proportion to the degree of limitation imposed upon its field of fact. Analytical realism aims to function effectively in direct proportion to its interpretative adequacy derived from a realistic comprehension of the functional unity within experience of form and fact. It seeks, further, for empirical adequacy beyond the abstractive domain of logico-empirical demonstrability, to which domain deduction and induction are both properly limited, by the inclusion of judgments which overarch formally tested factuality, and yet have the greatest possible degree of relevant and proportional relation to the realm of demonstrable certainty.

In order later to suggest a synthesis of the notions validity and adequacy, the growth of knowledge beyond that commonly experienced must be examined. The organic, functional interaction of form and fact can be seen in that new facts have suggested new forms and new forms have actually led to the discovery of new facts. By the mere study of forms relevant to astronomical theory a new planet was inductively established as a fact. The fact of a falling apple led to the understanding of the law of gravitation. The latter case falls within the field of uninterpreted experience; the former is a case of "cognitional creativity," of going beyond the observed realm of fact and form. The question at issue now is this: what is the philosophic status of any possible extension from experience? Every postulate is by nature lacking in present inductive verifiability. But this deficiency provides no valid ground for the positivistic denial of its rightfully possessed degree of reality. Knowledge grows by the extension of already established forms and by the attempt to ascertain the proper applicability of these extensions. Sometimes this can be done only by means of the effects, not immediately observable, of the facts indicated by the forms. If forms are the way facts function, the explanation of mere function is cognitionally inadequate. Yet functions indicate the presence of facts unknown in a strict sense, but nevertheless partially known through their relation with what is known. A good illustration is provided by theoretical physics, a proportionate extension of forms to explain certain effects on an already established realm of facts of interpreted experience. Its demonstrable certainty depends upon the expansion of knowledge by the manipulation of abstractions. Whenever extensions go beyond immediately verifiable experience they are deductive insofar as the process is concerned with the establishment of facts by means of abstract calculation from the forms already known. To assume that forms hold beyond the experience that we already know is not arbitrarily to accept a rational interpretation of the universe, for, as we have already found in many cases, as, for instance, in the discovery of a planet, the extension of forms may lead to the discovery of fact. We have no right, however, to say more than that these rational extensions from experience are probable in proportion to the factual applicability of the forms employed and to their correct abstract manipulation. Not until the fact is discovered, of course, can it have the same philosophic status as interpreted experience, but it has, nevertheless, a rightful claim to some degree of knowledge. In scientific theory the question is one of quantitative measurement, but, even so, in order adequately to explain its material, science advances beyond macroscopic equations, which are more readily tested, to microscopic and even to infra-microscopic equations. In the social sciences and religion, however, this farther reaching aspect of philosophic method is of utmost importance. The whole notion of going beyond that which can be readily and accurately tested for the sake of obtaining an adequate interpretation may perhaps, in view of its necessary relation to both forms and effects, be called "appropriate effectiveness." This notion has been introduced as one aspect of cognitional creativity. Appropriate effectiveness deals principally with what is already actual. Of utmost importance to social and religious theory, however, is the idea that inquiry and experiment, and even more, "the will to believe" as grounded faith, change the present social and religious attainment into a different situation. For this fact as well as for appropriate effectiveness the general idea of workability seems most suggestive.

We are left, therefore, with three tests for

philosophic truth: rational consistency, or coherence;[3] empirical applicability, or correspondence; and appropriate effectiveness, or, in a most guarded sense, workability. Because of the limited nature of the first two, appropriate effectiveness must be the philosophic method to provide adequate social and religious guidance in a day of change and confusion. Appropriate effectiveness combines as far as possible the two types of validity, while allowing ample room for social and religious adequacy.

From this point of view, however, is philosophy methodologically capable of arriving at any definiteness of interpretation? Is the total field of experience so comprehensive, are its data so complex in nature, are the limitations of each inquirer so constitutionally significant that only arbitrary systems of interpretation devoid of all objective validity can possibly result? Absolutism both of form and of content has been deemed impossible since all forms are extracted from experience. Skepticism is equally untenable. The legitimate scope of man's interpretative knowledge is neither all nor none. Such difficulties arise from

[3] "Coherence" can, of course, be used in a wider sense.

an absolutistic urge in man, the desire for unconditioned truth. Truth for us must be the correct
interpretation of experience inclusive of its possible implications. A little of the that and a little
of the how man seems to know; less he knows of
the what and the why. Dim is the distance beyond the life of man. His knowledge is touched
with all the contingency of experience. In its
light every theory is relative. Some theories seem
to possess more validity; some, more fullness.
Possibly certain aspects of experience can be
considered presuppositional for all human experience; but it seems arbitrary in the light of history
to limit all possible experience to the present
experience of human beings. Even in the case of
human experience, becoming as well as being
characterizes the forward plunging process; and
beyond the life of man, who dares to fix the absolute structure of experience? In his overcon-
fidence or fear, man makes universal assumptions,
valid not only for all times and spaces, but also
even beyond all times and spaces. But the dance
is still around the golden calf of man-made
abstractions.

Equally untenable is skepticism. Man knows

much, though exceedingly little. Psychological certitude may blind some to their lack of objective certainty; emotional frustration resulting from attempts to reach absolute knowledge leads others to the despairing affirmation of skepticism. Of the fullness of experience, however, man has gathered not a little understanding. Instead of accepting this as an obvious point of departure for further investigation and interpretation, supposedly wise men have been led away from the plains of increasing light by the road of doubt. When, if ever, they have at last returned from the dead-end of despair, they have come back with their increased critical capacity rendered almost useless by their defective sight which has prevented their unobstructed view of the experiential field. The way of detachment is the way of death. Isolation involves artificiality. If absolutism is impossible, skepticism is arbitrary. A certain relativism of man's knowledge seems inevitable, but man's relativity is not without structure, and much less is it chaotic.

Man thinks in small dimensions. What has he not learned in philosophy within the narrow limits of three thousand years? If only he could learn as much within a similar period in the future! What has not man learned in the realm of morality and religion within a period double that long? In spite of the present confusion, man's age-long quest for truth and goodness has not failed to leave significant results of ideals. Without pride, and conscious of constant failure, man can still assert that these ideals have received partial embodiment not only within his growing treasure of collective knowledge, but also in the lives which, when touched by them, have cherished them to the point of despair. What has not man learned in the realms of art, music, and literature within the last thousand years? In spite of the ugliness in much of modern art, in spite of the cacophony in much of modern music, in spite of the banality in much of recent literature, the last thousand years have produced creations to the legitimate delight of man. What has not man learned in the realm of the natural sciences within a period half that long? What has he not gained in historical insight within the last hundred years? It does not seem presumptuous to

[19]

claim that even within the narrow limits of this past generation man has learned a considerable amount which may not only increase the cumulative community of his knowledge, but also eventually help to interpret it. The astonishing technological discoveries may through abuse as well as through expedient use exert a directive influence on human history. Though dense is the distance of ignorance and dark are the depths of human potentiality, man has learned, by and large, surprisingly much within the brief span of recorded history.

A few suggestions follow from this study of knowledge as a social act. In the first place, all religious and social ideas must keep as close as possible to the reasoned interpretation of fact. The "existential involvement of things with one another," to use Dewey's phrase, must be a most important criterion of every social and religious theory. Interpretation, to be adequate in any field, ought to be as far as possible correctly and proportionately related to the cumulative verdict of social experience. Political despotism and religious fanaticism, unless they appeal to a limited and distorted reason, denounce the free use of it and resort to inherent right or alogical revelation. Social scientists and theologians have need of the insight that social adequacy, even though it goes beyond common, communicable certainty, is not devoid of reasoned validity but must avail itself of all the historical and rational interpretation at hand.

Particularly important in regard to the function of philosophy in these fields is the idea of inclusiveness. To whatever degree religion may be a matter of individual commitment to ideals, it has definite need of inclusiveness as a standard. Whitehead would say that the particularity of emotion requires the generality of thought. This idea is intensified, however, when it is remembered that knowledge is a social product and ought to be in social service. The ages have brought it into being and all the heirs of the ages ought to share in its benefits. In the social and religious sciences there is room for no interpretation in favor of a section of those involved in the present society of overlapping selves. All sectionalisms or sectarianisms which are invidious and

divisive in nature have no place in social and religious theory. Such use of philosophy is its abuse.
The generality of thought which characterizes
philosophic interpretation must be applied to the
entire field of philosophy. Ralph Barton Perry's
standard of inclusiveness in ethical theory is applicable to the fields of social and religious
thought as well; and his final solution seems experientially justified: "Upon the possibility of
benevolent cooperation repose whatever justifi-
able hopes there are of a constructive integration
of mankind, and of reconciling the full advan-
tage of united action with the prerogative of
personality."[4]

If our analysis of knowledge as a social act is
correct, moreover, it is evident that the primary
concern of social and religious theory must be
not validity but adequacy. Although adequacy is,
of course, never inconsistent with the fullest ascertainable validity, it extends beyond it. No one
lives by pure logic or by pure science. Logical inquiry and scientific experiment must be in the
service of life; and the logician and the scientist

[4] Perry, *A General Theory of Value*, p. 519.

ought to aid those interested in social research and guidance. In a strong society there must be no cleft between those whose task is primarily to establish validity and those whose first concern must be living meaningfulness. The former group ought to recognize that the latter tries to make its theories as valid as possible; and the logician and the scientist ought to try publicly to strengthen the hands of those who try intelligently to guide society. To fail to do so is to that extent to invite social demagogy and religious fanaticism. Religion, for instance, can use its power for good or ill. It can actively support social theories that make for freedom and faithfulness in fellowship; or it can sanction theories which deny it; or it can even deny the social quest altogether and thus hinder social advance. The deep powers of religion can be utilized to bring nearer the Kingdom of Ends. The best in democracy can be made more firm through religious support. More and more, bewildered social leaders are turning to religion to help preserve man's freedom. Only a religion which observes both the rules of validity and adequacy can do

[23]

this. To be preoccupied with the first is to invite meaninglessness and sterility; to be overly concerned with the second is to invite narrowness and fanaticism. Although logic must be primarily concerned with abstract validity, and science, with factual, social and religious theories must bravely endeavor to relate the ideal to the actual. They must leave the still waters of intellectual validity and venture out into the cross-currents of social conflict, to direct them, not so much by the certainties of existence as by the challenge of the ideal. It is, however, becoming increasingly obvious that neither science nor philosophy wishes with angelic watchfulness and the flaming sword of demonstrable validity to keep a bewildered human race from the garden of adequate social interpretation. The methodological appeal must be to what we have called "cognitional creativity" inclusive of appropriate effectiveness. Only by a resolute belief in the possibility of incarnating the ideal order can the actual order be changed. Every ideal can then be tested in relation to concrete human situations. Whatever helps man to free and peaceful concourse is that far real. Philosophy itself is making social adequacy more important by making the problem of values more central. If this interest, however, is not to degenerate into irrelevant disputation, social adequacy must itself become a criterion of truth.

The fact that knowledge is socially produced suggests, furthermore, that the best way to influence people is by means of historic beliefs. The way most people grow in insight is through the accustomed channels of community commitment. Although the cumulative ideals of a community are often distorted and destructive, the remedy lies not in the abandonment of the historic forms, but in their interpretation in more valid terms. The masses need the great seers, not to scorn their credulity, but sympathetically to aid them to see. To do so will require more than abstract investigation into specific fields of knowledge; it will mean the selection or production of symbols which can appeal to the whole man as a social being. These symbols must be selected with a view to their capacity for adequately relating the best of the past to the needs of the present. The way to help people become socially and religiously more adequate is not to uproot them from their historic faith and transplant them to a new ideology, but to nurture them in their accustomed soil. Whitehead is undoubtedly right in claiming that "the successful adaptation of old symbols to changes of social structure is the final mark of wisdom in sociological statesmanship."[5] Philosophy and theology must not only clear away useless or detrimental symbolism, but they must also provide society with those true symbols that can vitally affect social conduct. In critical epochs civilization is desperately in need of realistic thinkers who are actively concerned with the problems of humanity. To-day is such a period. Concerted efforts among those who possess meaningful insights can alone provide for the better life.

Our investigation ought also to throw some light on the present growing conflict between the philosophy of religion and theology. Many modern thinkers repudiate theology altogether because of what seems its arbitrary claim to be a special kind of truth. Others are rapidly turning

[5] Whitehead, *Symbolism, Its Meaning and Effect*, p. 61.

away from the philosophy of religion because they feel that speculative philosophy can never by itself find the Christian Revelation. Our study ought to reveal that both positions contain needed truth. Not to admit that there is something given in history is to be unrealistic. Through certain individuals something new breaks into the previous situation which mere thought is unable to account for except as emergence. To suppose that by explaining knowledge as a social act we have also accounted for its origin is to have committed the genetic fallacy; it is fallaciously to have identified product with process. The new may be explained in terms of emergence or of revelation depending upon whether the problem is approached from the naturalistic or from the supernaturalistic point of view. If the former view can claim economy of interpretation, the latter fulfils far better the principle of sufficient reason. It seems unlikely that individual speculation can achieve any important discovery of truth unless it be in touch with a greater reality than itself and its natural world.

Perhaps all significant newness in history

ought to be thought of in terms of revelation. Theology is right, in any case, in its insistence on the fact that its faith is not merely the result of rational thought; it is not merely a human discovery concerning our natural world. The philosophy of religion, on the other hand, safeguards another important insight. The new light of revelation would be but a flicker in time unless it became continued as a social act. Only because it meets certain rational and experiential needs does revelation pass beyond the individual and remain as a social act. D. G. Moses is entirely right in his distinction between the antecedent and the consequent reason. Antecedent to its arrival the revelation is inaccessible to reason; consequent to it, however, it can be understood and verified both in thought and in life. Those who believe in theology as the only method of dealing with Christian faith, who insist on the givenness of Revelation as inaccessible to rational or experiential verification, must remember, moreover, that to most earnest thinkers outside the theological field their claims look arbitrary. Theologians ought to show some reason for the faith

[28]

that is in them. Even faith must be firmly grounded. There is thus a real need for competent philosophy of religion.

If the thesis of this chapter is correct, however, it also provides a foundation for theology. Adequate reasoning must have a historical content and must be built on faith. The general truths of experience, moreover, do not provide either the ideal or the power necessary for the salvation of the individual or of the world. Christian theology is built on a common, continuous commitment to a special truth and power which came into the world through Jesus Christ. That this Revelation possesses both validity and adequacy we shall try to illustrate in the next chapter. The social act which is theology can thus claim a historic basis which is at the same time universal and ultimate in nature. The final acceptance of this basis, however, must be an individual act. Religious knowledge needs a firm historical foundation, but in the last analysis the verification of its relevancy lies with the individual. Its standard cannot be empirical demonstrability or even common communicability and in-

clusiveness. Only personal adequacy will do. The
ideal and the power to realize that ideal must become a matter of personal concern. The adequate relation of the individual to the ultimate
Reality is beyond full common communicability. To reduce faith to philosophic verifiability
is to surrender that special Revelation of the ideal
through which alone the actual world can be
saved. Inclusiveness is a useless standard for theology. The ultimate appeal of *the* faith must be
to faith.

It is our contention that when the historic
Christian faith becomes alive in personal faith it
is both fact-finding and fact-making. It finds a
religious ultimate by means of which it can make
a new actuality, a new fact. The just shall truly
live by faith. This truth judges both the philoso-
phers who want to build Christian faith entirely
on rational demonstrability in the light of this
actual world and also those theologians who de-
clare that *the* faith is unconditioned by faith, that
Revelation is independent of human reason or
experience. Whatever be true of the historic
giving of the Revelation, apart from knowledge

[30]

as a social act, Christian faith would not be operative today. Christian knowledge as a social act is unrealistic and ineffective unless it make the Revelation in Jesus Christ ultimate; but its commitment ought to be based on its living experience that its faith can, in the fullness of time, by providing the highest rational ideal and the source of power to effect it, become universally realized.

II

The Unity and Continuity of the Christian Faith

IF WE turn our attention to contemporary theology, what do we find? Liberal theology is weakened by vagueness. Its content of faith is too general to be deeply convincing. Because it has no adequate understanding of its own nature, it has no clear principle of exclusion. Its inclusive generosity is often little more than a lack of vigorous spiritual discrimination. Its tolerance cannot be fully divorced from a lack of intense conviction. In revolting from an inadequate supernaturalism, liberal thought, to no small measure, has become indefinite, negative, and ineffective. Much of its social drive is the expenditure of spiritual capital inherited from generations of conservative Christian background, much of it being, in fact, an attempt to satisfy the hunger for a definite faith with the substitute of humanitarian activities. Traditional theology, on the other hand, has been to a great extent defensive rather than constructive, worshipping the letter to the detriment of the spirit. Its deep commitment to the essentials of Christian faith has made for an emotional conservatism which has kept many a fundamentalist thinker from facing squarely the issues raised by modern scholarship. It is the writer's belief that traditional theology can keep the substance of its faith and still be more intellectually and socially effective, and that liberalism can keep its intellectual and social passion and at the same time obtain a more adequate and definite standard of faith—when and insofar as the nature of Christian faith is itself understood. Traditional theology and liberalism are fully compatible when what is contingent in both is resolutely cleared away. The result is then not the lowest denominator of positive faith, but the highest plus all the richness which both sides can contribute.

To be at all definite, Christian faith must have some principle of unity and continuity. Practically all Christians agree that in some sense this principle is Jesus Christ. The danger of emphasizing the Lordship of Christ without defining it is that it may be reduced to an ineffective, individualistic relativism. To make this emphasis, in fact, is no better than to attribute everything indiscriminately to the will of God. Many able thinkers are of the opinion that the unity and continuity of the Christian faith is specious rather than real. They hold that Jesus is only the symbol of a certain idealism, the content of which can change and has changed from place to place and from age to age. The life and teachings of Jesus thus provide nothing more than a specious unity because those who claim to follow him differ in their interpretation both of what he was and of what he taught. The continuity is likewise specious, and even more so, because new eras put different interpretations on their common Master.

It is not enough, therefore, to claim real unity and continuity for the Christian faith merely because of common allegiance to a common Lord. This claim needs both definition and historic attestation. Several methods of confirming it have,

[34]

of course, been attempted. The most impressive of these, perhaps, is the doctrine of the Roman Catholic Church. Jesus, the supernatural Son of God, imparted certain teachings and made possible certain means of grace, which he entrusted to an infallible Church. The supernatural nature of Jesus was confirmed by miracles which were witnessed to by multitudes still living at the time when the earliest records of Christian faith were written. The founding of the Church to guard the Gospel is itself recorded within these writings. The unity and continuity of the Christian faith is constituted by an infallible Revelation of a sufficient, supernatural Redemption continuously disclosed and made available through an infallible Church.

As an ideal this view is exceedingly strong. Actually, however, there are a number of points which make it unacceptable: the results of Biblical scholarship, the history of Christianity, the sectarian position the view now involves, and possibly its inapplicable use of Platonic philosophy. New Testament scholars, if they admit, as some of the ablest do not, that Jesus founded a church at all, generally agree that the church he founded was not the kind of church which Roman Catholicism has gradually evolved. When the history of Christianity is studied carefully, the Roman Church is seen to be a historic development considerably patterned upon the Roman Empire and explainable to a great degree by certain historic conditions. Its position is now exclusive, not by virtue of the essence of Christianity, but by virtue of its absolutizing certain doctrines developed through the history of its struggles to maintain the unity and continuity of the Christian faith. By limiting the full reality of the Christian fellowship to a certain historic organization, which is clearly *de facto* but a part of it, the Roman Church has become a sect. This may, to a great extent, be due to its use of Platonic philosophy which has made it identify the visible Church, in the manner of conceptual realism, with the eternal idea of the true Church in such a way as to rule out *a priori* the existence of the Christian Church beyond its own temporal organization. Since the Roman Church, in general, considers itself indispensable to salvation because of its exclusive possession of the means of grace, the inadequacy of its position is vividly revealed by the very essence of Christian faith which is also clearly manifest outside it. While the Roman Catholic Church has the idea of the unity and continuity of the Christian faith expressed in doctrines which in spite of their historic forms witness to vital and much neglected truths, it nevertheless suffers from its absolutizing of contingent, historic instrumentalities.

A second method of emphasizing and of conserving the unity and continuity of the Christian faith is the one which makes central the Bible as the record of the Christian Revelation. If Jesus is the foundation of the Christian faith, and if the Bible is the only adequate account of his life and teachings, why is not the best possible religion that of the Bible? The Bible, too, open to any one, presents a direct personal way to the knowledge of God's Revelation in Jesus Christ.

It is, naturally, at once obvious and beyond dispute that if there is a real unity and continuity of the Christian faith, the record of it must be found unmistakably in the Bible. In a most im-

[37]

portant way Christianity is by its very nature inevitably the religion of the Bible. Just as, in the case of the Roman Church, however, despite its strong position in its doctrine of the Church as the infallible guard, interpreter, and necessary agent of the Christian Revelation, we cannot accept its emphasis on the institution itself because it is a destructive and divisive absolutizing of the historically conditioned, so and for the same reason we cannot be satisfied with the religion of the Book. In view of the varied contents of the Bible, to call it equally and infallibly inspired seems something of idolatry. The position, though devout and expressive of man's desire for a definite hold on the absolute, nevertheless contains an inherent inadequacy. It lacks discrimination. To make the whole Bible of equal authority throughout is to rob it of its full power. God makes Abraham sacrifice even Isaac, His own gift according to the promise, when Isaac takes the place of God. The Giver is more than the gift; the spirit, than the letter. But besides, the historical sciences, which first came to critical maturity with the beginning of the nineteenth century, revealed both development within the thought of the Bible and the reception of ideas into the Judeo-Christian tradition from outside sources; they revealed, in short, the human conditionedness of the Bible. It seems certain that in wide circles of Christianity from liberalism to Barthianism literalism is being more and more abandoned. The literalistic position was particularly destructive because it made for an increasing number of sects each taking literally some teaching in the Bible which others insisted had a merely figurative significance. Literalism is automatically divisive, especially without a firm organ of authority to rule on various interpretations. Many of those who wish to find in the Bible itself the unity and continuity of the Christian faith are now turning to Biblical realism which affirms the uniqueness and absoluteness of the Christian faith revealed through the Bible as a whole without rejecting entirely the findings of analytical criticism. A synthetic method of historical interpretation, greatly needed, is beginning to take the place, in large areas, of an inadequate Biblical literalism. Good as this is, however, it cannot by itself answer the claim on the part of Christian faith to have a real unity and continuity. The content of this claim must be defined, tested historically, and, if possible, verified by reason and in experience.

Another movement emphasizing the unity and continuity of the Christian faith is that of Dialectic Theology. Here the unity is in no sense immanent in history, not even in the Bible. Its only principle is the transcendent Will of God, once and only once fully revealed in Jesus, the Word of God, but understandable through God's grace in the existential situation, in the crushed soul realizing its utter helplessness, in the experience where, as Gogarten puts it, we stand stark naked before God. The unity and continuity of the Christian faith is really the ever-deciding Will of God working in history, though not through human history, to save through Christ those who are to be saved. It is the activity of God's Holy Spirit, beyond the ways of man and nature and contrary to all reason and desert, to save those who find or are found by the Only Way to be reconciled with a God Wholly Other than the speculations, plans, and desires of men. The abiding essence of Christianity, as Barth never fails to stress, is Jesus Christ, but it is not for man as man to understand. The objective Revelation of God in Jesus Christ, witnessed to by the Bible and the Creeds, the testifying symbols of Christian faith, is ever and ever a divine mystery beyond the rational comprehension of man, and must be received, to use Barth's phrase, pneumatically or not at all. There is thus a permanent sameness in Christian faith, according to Dialectic Theology, which, although it has been objectively disclosed by means of a concrete divine Act in history, nevertheless cannot be understood apart from God's direct revelation through His Holy Spirit.

Valuable is the stress of this view on the divine initiative, on the fact that in the last analysis God Himself constitutes the unity and continuity of the Christian faith. Here also is confident understanding of the uniqueness and absoluteness of Christianity, which even though it fails to provide an adequate principle of inclusion, at least helpfully indicates the weakness of a liberal theology fed on a vague idealism without a strong principle of exclusion. The stress, too, on the centrality of the Christ-deed, on man's need to surrender himself completely to God before he can know Him, and the emphasis that both this surrender and the experience of being found by God are ultimately due to the grace of God— all this is part and parcel of vital Christianity. The real fault of this view, however, is that it leaves us with an arbitrary view of God in the name of divine freedom, while it also robs man of that responsibility and personal reality which alone can make any measure of fellowship meaningful. Its denial of the rational and experiential verification of religion is also arbitrary, and destructive of the fullest inclusiveness of the religious realm. We must always remember, however, that the Dialectic theologians face a concrete situation where pragmatic considerations play a great part. In private they may admit that Brunner's position, for instance, is a more adequate interpretation, but that because it opens the door to naturalistic and rationalistic thought it is dangerous to the European churches in their life-

and-death struggle with paganism. With all sympathy, therefore, and without winking at the inadequacies, we can summarize their view of the unity and continuity of the Christian faith as prophetic, as God's direct and exclusive dealing with the world through His chosen, as the prophetic witnessing, without regard for interpretative adequacy, to the all-sufficiency and all-importance of God's redemptive work through His Son.

A new movement to interpret the unity and continuity of the Christian faith is under way. Although this view claims to make Christ central, he is so not through any specific act or teaching but through the kind of fellowship that he founded. Indeed, the very doctrine of Christ is itself the product of that organic unity and continuity which the Christian community is. In other words, the doctrines themselves are considered of secondary importance, being continuously created by that primary reality which is the Christian Church. This view does not hesitate to call the Christian faith both unique and absolute, but the uniqueness and absoluteness of the faith is the Christian community itself as a distinct organism chosen by God for man's salvation.

This position has a real sense of history. It appreciates a special history of revelation and redemption within general history. Jesus is lifted, moreover, from the particularities of the peculiar history of his time and made into an effective Christ of faith working continuously through his Body, the Holy Church. Those who hold this view are taking the work of the Holy Spirit in earnest and are not willing to restrict God's revelation to the past. His revelation to-day and to-morrow is not merely the explanation of what He has said before, but a new and vital imparting of Himself. The interpretation accounts for many problems of historical scholarship otherwise left unexplained or left entirely to human creativity. Doctrines have been developed beyond those taught explicitly by Jesus. Especially is this true if much in the New Testament is considered to be the teachings of the Early Church. The interpretation also has abundant capacity for continuous adjustment to new historic situations. Nor is its unity specious, for it is as real as the organic nature of any living society. At the same time this community is by its very nature, since the intellectual affirmations are of secondary importance, capable of including wide differences of interpretation, as wide, in fact, as the organic unity of the ongoing Christian community itself. There is thus much in this view which is true, much in it which must be heavily emphasized as against all static views of the Christian faith; but at the same time there is also much in it which is dangerously untrue. Modern pragmatism has developed an operational view in which the *a priori* rises out of experience in the long run; but, even so, by becoming a conventional mode of interpretation, it becomes definitional, that is, presuppositional in the sense that no explanation in the present can be given apart from that socially created *a priori* which alone makes possible common communicability and understanding. What we know is to be defined in no sense in terms of ultimate metaphysical laws valid apart from a social matrix of interpretation, but only in and through this. Some objective reality there is apart from social definition, but our knowledge of this reality is through and through conditioned by the very way in which mankind has come to look at its world. In other words, the way of looking is conventional, not objectively and ultimately necessary. The whole position can be summarized by our saying that the unity is a cumulative, conventional, hypothetical, presuppositional, definitional, social creation!

It is, of course, immediately obvious from even a cursory comparison that if we interpret the Christian fellowship as central to the Christian faith, we have succumbed to a secular anti-intellectualism which is inconsistent with the historic nature of Christianity. However worthy is the intent to make the Christian fellowship primary rather than a system of ideas, the Christian religion has something given in its Revelation which contains eternal truth beyond the relative and changing interpretations of men. It refers to an order of Reality beyond man's conventional creations. It insists that God is not merely a principle of creativity, expressing Himself in His highest new creation in the Christian Church, but that God's Will contains some eternal order, that the content of His creation is not devoid of fixity of form. Whatever is said of the religion of the infallible Church or of the infallible Book, both claiming to transmit without error the faith once-for-all delivered to the saints, both of these two great approaches guard the truth that there is not only faith in fellowship, but also a fellowship of faith. There is, in short, not only Christian faith, but also *the* Christian faith.

What unity and continuity of the Christian faith can there be, however, apart from an infallible Church or an infallible Book guarding a given Revelation; or apart from the transcendent Will of God itself, revealed in Jesus Christ, at least sufficiently unto salvation, to those who are found by the Holy Spirit; or apart from living fellowship continuously loyal to Christ even though itself constituting the principle of permanent sameness? It is the writer's claim that Christian faith has an ascertainable basis in history while it is at the same time verifiable both by reason and in experience. The unity and continuity of Christian faith is historically given,

[47]

is man's highest applicable ideal, and has been and can be tested by any one willing to accept it.

It seems an undeniable fact of history that through Jesus there came into full historical awareness the idea of Christian love, the love which seeketh not its own, the love which has its source and standard in God ("Be ye therefore perfect, even as your Father . . ."), the love which transcends the worth of its object, the love which centers its attention exclusively on the welfare of others, the love which creates fellowship because it is based not on need but on strength, the love which gives its life even for its enemies. "Love your enemies . . . and ye shall be sons of the Most High: for he is kind toward the unthankful and evil." It is our conviction that this kind of love is the determinative, distinctive motif of Christianity, that it constitutes its ultimate principle of explanation in the light of which all doctrines are to be defined and by means of which they are most adequately understood. Such a contention naturally needs historical confirmation. If it is found historically to be the essence of Christianity, it then needs the attestation of reason and experience.

Our first question is whether the New Testament kind of love, *agape*, is the determinative motif of Christianity. This question will be more carefully discussed in a separate chapter where Professor Anders Nygren's outstanding work, *Agape and Eros*, the history of the Christian idea of love, is appraised. At this point, however, it is necessary to say that when we call the Christian kind of love a determinative motif of Christianity we mean that it is so essential to Christianity, so central to its understanding, that without it Christianity cannot be adequately understood, and more, that there is no idea besides it through which Christianity can be better explained. *Agape* constitutes Christianity's ultimate principle of interpretation. The basic relation between God and man, according to Christian faith, is the kind of love that freely gives itself regardless of the merit of its object. God loves both the good and the evil. The father stands ready to receive his prodigal son, while all that he has belongs at the same time to the elder brother. The good shepherd seeks the lost sheep. The Samaritan takes pity even on the Jew. The follower of Jesus must accept the cross of redemptive love. He must, indeed, love even his enemies.

Indeed, this idea of love is the key to Christian theology. God is a redeeming love who so loved the world that He gave His own Son. John could even write that God is love and he that loves his brother in this way is born of God. *Agape* is the test both of our knowledge of God and of our sonship. Paul reaches the height of Christian ethics in his great hymn of love where if love is absent everything is declared worthless. This ethics he derived directly from his view of God as redeeming the world through the Christ. Those who use this key will find in the New Testament a profound agreement far deeper than the divergent interpretations.

Jesus, too, is best understood through this motif. Scholars say that there were in the Early Church three interpretations of Jesus. He was the Son of God in the sense that he was actually God; he was a prophet; he was the Word of God with all the possible explanations that this philosophic position involved. To-day these three dominant positions still stand. One thing, however, must unite them all as the early disciples were united: God was this love which Jesus proclaimed and lived, and only in terms of it can Jesus be explained. He is the revelation in life and teaching, in being and message, of the ultimate principle of all explanation. To sever the importance of Jesus from the Deepest Reality in the universe is to become theologically inadequate. Let the different faiths interpret him differently in other respects, but this one thing is essential. With Jesus enters both as life and as light that full *agape* which is the key to Christian doctrine and gives us our deepest understanding of God. The God who was this kind of love and who dealt with the world through it must at the last be victorious. The pictures of this victory differed, but the victory itself was certain. Thus became joined in Christian faith the cross and the crown, the fellowship of his suffering and the power of his resurrection. The central symbols of Christian faith are the Incarnation of this redemptive Love, the Cross, and the empty Tomb.

[51]

However interpretations of these deep realities may differ, without a firm faith in their ultimacy there is not vital Christianity. Any new orthodoxy must at bottom be the old orthodoxy, a new rendering of "the old, old story." Liberal, fundamentalist, or essentialist—all must subscribe to the central unity and continuity of the Christian faith or be outside its pale. Christianity has a definite principle both of inclusion and of exclusion. "This is the condemnation, that light is come into the world. . . ."

Although much more must be said on this theme later, one caution must be given here. When it is claimed that the New Testament idea of love is the determinative principle of Christianity, this principle is in no sense equated with either the ideological or the sociological history of Christianity. The essence of Christian faith cannot be extracted from the Bible if a literal infallibility is maintained. Many ideas in the New Testament are either contrary to or not fully up to the level of this idea. A specific investigation must deal with this problem. This idea of God as redemptive love is there, however, as the central core of the New Testament and of the history of Christian thought. Remove it from the Christian writings, from sermons and hymns, from symbols and confessions, as well as from its explicit theologies, and the essence of the Christian Gospel, the mystery beyond man's rational knowledge and natural conduct, the unity and continuity of the Christian faith is gone. The caution, therefore, is this: when we say that the New Testament idea of love is the determinative motif of Christian faith, we mean that it constitutes its very essence in the light of which the several Christian doctrines can best be understood. This determinative motif is thus normative for Christianity, but Christians have failed to understand, to believe in and effectively to incarnate normative Christianity. The phenomenological approach is not, therefore, empirical if it is only traditionally descriptive in the sense of what most Christians have thought and lived. When Christian faith as expressed in the New Testament, however, is understood and practiced, its idea of love is ever determinative. Christianity is the kind of community which re-

sults from the experience of this love. It is a freedom and faithfulness in fellowship, centered in
God, and first fully revealed as life and light
through Jesus Christ.

Since our claim that this kind of love is distinctive to Christianity must be more fully discussed in a later chapter, we need only point out
in this connection that there is something unique
in Christianity. This is not a philosophic theory,
but a historic fact. In no place outside Christianity, at least not until Christianity made its revelation available, has the Christian idea of fellowship
through God's redemptive love been a determinative notion. There are ideas which approach it,
even outside the Old Testament; but, as we shall
see, they are not the fullness of God's revelation
in Christ Jesus. Christianity is founded on something objectively given. It is rooted in history.
The importance of the historical Jesus is not understood until he becomes the Christ of faith.
Because Jesus both in life and in teachings is the
founder of the Christian faith, because he both
incarnated and taught it, he is the Church's one
foundation, but not apart from the Father, the

very Source and Standard of *agape*. Nor, again, is the Revelation in Jesus unique in the sense that it cannot be understood or verified. On the very contrary, through it we can best understand the world in which we live and the experience which is ours.

The Christian ideal of fellowship can be tested both as a rational ideal and as a historic fact. After this is done, we can ask concerning its claim to be the ultimate principle of explanation. Does Christianity provide the highest ideal that can be thought by man? An ideal can be tested only in the light of its capacity to satisfy the deepest needs of man. The Christian ideal is freedom and faithfulness of fellowship based on the kind of love first fully revealed and made effective as light and life in Jesus Christ, a fellowship which is through and through centered and stayed in God. Is this what man must have to find his deepest satisfaction? There can be no question that men long to be free. Without an element of freedom, life becomes dull and oppressive. Yet freedom apart from faithfulness is most unsatisfactory. Among the most unhappy people in the world are those who have their freedom but nothing to do with it. Dictatorships flourish when liberalism releases men from bondage and gives them a freedom which soon becomes meaningless. To be free men must be faithful. To be strong selves they must have loyalties. These loyalties, moreover, are never fully satisfactory when they are to things and principles and not to personalities. As Aristotle long ago pointed out and as the whole of experience has confirmed, men are naturally social beings. Apart from fellowship there is no abiding satisfaction. Even the mystic, as Hocking says, has a need for the community. The hermit's life is not without a social reference. One of the worst forms of punishment is solitary confinement. Without love every life has an aching void. Those who have never fully surrendered to the experience of love do not know the depths of life.

The freedom and faithfulness in fellowship for which man yearns, however, is impossible apart from the kind of love which Christianity demands. Not every kind of togetherness satisfies. There are low forms of fellowship, possessing some liberty and loyalty, but which still by their inadequacy burden the heart. Communities held together by enlightened selfishness lead lives which are lonely and dissatisfied. There can be neither full freedom nor faithfulness in fellowship apart from the love of Christ. We Christians have in our Gospel, not some incomprehensible secret, but an open message which can be tested by reason. While we bask in indifference or spend our time in proving unessentials, the world is accepting other loyalties, for loyalties it must have. These loyalties, too, must be rooted in the very nature of things. Man is naturally religious, and his deepest convictions have a cosmic reference. Religion is man's concern for the conditions in the universe which make possible his deepest desire, his freedom and faithfulness in fellowship.

Perhaps we can sum up our argument that Christianity is man's highest ideal in this way. To be happy a man must be free, and he cannot be free without voluntary loyalties. Freedom without faithfulness soon becomes void and destructive. The monotony of empty freedom drives men to relieve it in many evil forms from peevishness to war. Neither liberty nor loyalty, moreover, is ever fully realized apart from a fellowship motivated by good will. When, however, man's fellowship becomes of intense concern to him he cannot help being interested in the cosmic conditions which make that fellowship possible. Thus Dewey defines God as the element in the universe which makes possible the progress of ideals. And ideals are always in and for a social continuum. Hocking defines religion as man's passion for righteousness, and for the spread of righteousness, with a cosmic guarantee. Religion is a matter of human fellowship, not alone, but with the conditions in the universe on which it depends. The Christian answer to this cosmic quest is that God is Himself the kind of love which makes possible freedom and faithfulness in fellowship. As a rational ideal, therefore, as a historic hypothesis first offered by Jesus, and that mostly in the form of parables, as nothing more than this, Christianity fulfils the deepest desires and needs of man. Christianity is the key to an ideal civilization, for it opens the way to the only kind of community in which man can find permanent and full satisfaction. Christianity affirms that free creativity and voluntary loyalty to the kind of community motivated by good will are man's highest ideal. Even more, it claims this to be the final principle of interpretation of the world in which we live.

That this is so we aim to illustrate more fully in the next chapter. Before entering into more detail, however, as to the meaning of history in terms of fellowship, or of Christianity in terms of the most intensive kind of such fellowship, topics to which we shall devote the next two chapters, it is well to give the gist of the argument in this connection to suggest how Christianity has a basic relation to history as a whole and how all of history witnesses to the ultimate truth of the Christian faith.

There can be no question that through even our short history there has been growth in the extensive modes of human togetherness. Men have advanced from food-finders to food-producers. They have passed from family to tribe to nation and almost to world citizens. This they have done without conscious planning but as a result of the forces of history. Hunger made food producing necessary. Whether new activities made for new abilities or new abilities for new activities, both increased perceptibly. When man became a food-producer he began to acquire property. First domesticated cattle and pasture lands gradually united a few into a tribal mode of life. Or in hunting communities the weapons were the means and media of man's togetherness. Then slowly arose trade, in crude forms, to be sure; yet trade enlarged man's mental horizons, extended the boundaries of the community of which he was aware. Soon property and trade required more extensive organization and even armies to protect them. Man's extensive modes of fellowship grew by the media of his fellowship. Technological progress tended, if not to unite men, at least to enlarge the scope of the communities of interest. This theme could be illustrated in almost countless ways, but it is sufficient to mention the discovery of fire, the development of language, the invention of the alphabet, the use of the printing press, the compass, steam, the telegraph, the aeroplane, the radio. How can one trace the rapid rate of progress in the technological sense in the short history of our little world? Not man's conscious planning, but the very nexus of history larger than man made for a rapid growth in the human community. Was not this progress related to a purpose? If so, how?

Man's needs are more than the physical. Man shall not live by bread alone. On the psychological level there is the need for companionship. This usually has been best realized through media. Most of us feel like sharing a good book, a noble friend, a challenging cause. In common quest for beauty men have been drawn together all over the world. The history of expansion of interest shows more than those interests based only on commercial needs. The economic interpretation of history is only partial truth. Literature, art, and the pursuit of many ideals have brought men together, and as the means of communication and travel have expanded, so the knowledge and appreciation of common ideals, interests, and commitments have spread over the whole world.

Even here technological discoveries have helped to stimulate interest, and the media of fellowship have played a large part beyond any conscious planning of man. A Titian goes to the Netherlands; Americans used to go to Salzburg. The quest for truth brings scholars and educators together throughout large and sometimes world communities. The psychological needs for companionship in the pursuit of the ideal, particularly by means of external media, have thus helped to expand man's extensive modes of fellowship.

The same can be said of man's spiritual needs. Religion has taken many forms. Primitive men reacted in their way to the forces which they thought ruled the world about them. The tribes had their tribal rites. As the external modes of togetherness grew, however, religious thought forms also grew to fit the new and larger loyalties. Thus the local deities gave way to national gods, while these in turn left their origin and, according to their capacity to satisfy larger views, grew with the growth in man's extensive forms of fellowship. To-day we have, in general, national religions and world religions facing each other. Our problem is coming to be how to fit the local religions into the world religions, and then how to determine which is to remain as the ultimate religion of a rapidly uniting world. Our thought can hardly follow the growth of world-consciousness in recent centuries, so rapid has it been. We are also on the threshold of large transformations even with regard to the religions of the world, which have corresponded to a large extent with the needs of the people. The great need of man for cosmic adjustment has taken form much in accordance with the historic fellowship out of which each religion has risen. Buddhism is, to a great extent, a fellowship of suffering, but with changing conditions and in the healthy life of the people its negativism has often been greatly modified in a positive direction. Confucian ethics has needed the supplement of Taoist mysticism or Buddhist metaphysics. On all levels of life, on the religious as well as the technological and the social, there has been this progress in the external modes of togetherness. The forms of man's fellowship by means of his needs and *without his conscious guidance* have become more and more extensive.

The important thing about this progress in the

[63]

extensive forms of fellowship, moreover, is that it has suggested the need of intensive forms. Mere need is insufficient to let man live happily. Progress by itself can become demonic and thwart purpose. The ultimate criterion of the kind of fellowship man is to have is spiritual. Thus man discovers the use of steam; but this can be used either to carry scientists to a significant conference or to propel a warship. Discoveries in chemistry may heal aching bodies or poison millions in war. Automobiles may carry angels of mercy and yet introduce moral and family problems. What is good as a means and a medium of fellowship can be perverted, but as a whole the history of progress shows that the extensive modes of man's togetherness have suggested and made possible the intensive forms of fellowship without which the extensive cannot be more than thinly good. History is ultimately a spiritual affair. The story of progress, therefore, indicates a Purpose, not of coercion but of leading men to the light. It is said that history is slow but sure. When we see history as but a day that is past we are amazed at the Purpose revealed in our little time. On one

side it is a rough purpose. What can be less sentimental than actual history? Yet it is not without
an aim. Even wars are tokens that history cannot
stop the pulsing power of God's purpose. Communities must at least become vitally aware of
each other. Since indifference and ignorance
make fellowship impossible, even wars help to
make men conscious of each other and to see the
need for the intensive modes of fellowship without which the world cannot get along.

Consider the intensive modes of fellowship on
the lower level. Man has not only hunger as a
basic drive, but also the need to perpetuate his
species. This need has led to the creation of the
family and all the possibilities for intimate fellowship which it affords. With regard to the
deeper basis of family life, moreover, the Freudians are right in their refusal to localize sex as a
specific physical function. We have even within
our natural needs drives which open up the possibility for intensive fellowship and which have
often led to the deepest experiences of fellowship
afforded to man. The family has thus become a
symbol for the Christian religion in which we

[65]

even speak of the Fatherhood of God and the brotherhood of man.

Yet life is not entirely a matter of need in the sense of disturbed equilibrium, but can also be a matter of overflowing strength. Let us return in this connection to the unity and continuity of Christianity. The basic truth of Christian faith, its ultimate principle of explanation, we found to be freedom and faithfulness in fellowship based on the kind of love first fully revealed and made effective as light and life in Jesus Christ. The whole trend of history, its entire purpose, seems to be to bring this about. What history reveals as man's universally most basic need, Christianity offers as a positive gift. Christian faith is thus not only the clue but the answer to history. The extensive forms of fellowship have developed through a history of progress beyond the conscious planning of man. These extensive forms, moreover, have revealed the need for an intensive form, for a spiritual dynamic, for a positive disposition creative of good will, for an inner power of transforming and rightly using the means and media of fellowship lest they become demonic,

[66]

lest they thwart and destroy even the fellowship which man now has. The Christian faith is the answer to the world's problem. That Purpose which has been working through progress suggesting to man that he find and accept the intensive forms has also given the answer in Jesus Christ. In his Revelation, in his Gospel, is man's only way to full salvation. Other foundation can no man lay, for it answers both the deepest need of man and explains the superhuman currents of history.

Purpose works through progress to suggest and make possible by man's needs in terms of his larger horizons a higher form of fellowship. There is also another stream in history: the intensive form of fellowship issuing from Jesus' life and based on his love. This positive answer is the Christian Church. He who does not have the Church for his mother, as Cyprian said, cannot have God for his Father. *Extra ecclesiam nulla salus*. This is true because the Christian Church is that ultimate kind of fellowship which wherever it is found represents the creative purpose of God as far as we human beings can see at all and without which man can find no abiding peace. The continuity and unity of the Christian faith are through the Christian Church as a living organic fellowship witnessing to the revelation in Christ. This fellowship is, in truth, the extension of the Incarnation. Insofar as this stream of intensive fellowship is vital, warmed by the very spirit of Christ, the Holy Spirit of God working in the world, it must transform the world both at home and abroad. In the Christian faith we have an absolute answer to the world's problems. Missions whether at home or abroad are the positive proclaiming of God's answer in history through Jesus Christ, the answer needed to the growth of man's external forms of togetherness. Creation without redemption is accursed. Man needs the light and power from the God who made him in order to understand the nature of technological and social progress and to use it in the service of fellowship. God's purpose is working in history and in nature.[1] His Church is failing to do its part in letting God redeem through it His creation. In the kind of fellowship which a Church

[1] An analysis of nature would further confirm this thesis.

worshipping in the spirit of Christ can effect lies the answer to the world's deepest problem.

The burden of this chapter is to point out that the Christian faith has a unity and continuity historically ascertainable. The essence of Christianity is a kind of fellowship which humanly speaking, at least, is both distinctive and final. This faith, too, is both metaphysically grounded and also rationally and experientially verifiable. This chapter has suggested one approach to verify it. History shows us a Purpose working through the push of progress to suggest to man his need for the Christian fellowship, but it also reveals the pull of its Purpose as revealed in Jesus Christ. Only by a clear understanding of its nature can Christianity come to that unity, that synthesis of both extensive and intensive forms of fellowship, through which the Church can transform the world.

III

The Basis of Christian Fellowship

IN THE preceding chapter we mentioned besides the extensive modes of fellowship the specifically intensive mode based on *agape* as revealed and made effective through Jesus Christ. This idea of *agape* has been scholarly set forth by Professor Anders Nygren of Lund University. There can be no question that Nygren's investigations into Christianity as *agape* constitute one of the most important contributions in the history of theological thought. His works are winning immediate recognition among thorough and open-minded thinkers. It is very fortunate that the third part of his *Agape and Eros, the History of the Christian Idea of Love* has now appeared in English, for in several ways this section is of basic importance to the rest of his investigations. Especially should his analysis of Augustine's treatment of love, a most careful, enlightening, and immensely stimulating study, be carefully considered by every one who is interested in the nature of Christianity. The writer's own feeling after reading the complete work *Agape and Eros* was that it was an investigation of such depth and significance of insights as to deserve a place among the great books of theology. Several years of working with its problems have only confirmed, rather than weakened, this opinion.

To facilitate the understanding of the attempt to appraise Christianity as *agape*, we may resort to a brief summary of Nygren's doctrine.[1] The uniqueness of Christianity lies in its basic motif, in its picture of God as *agape*. *Agape* is God's way to man; *eros* is man's way to God. Jesus broke with Judaism when he spoke of God's calling not the righteous, but sinners; when he spoke of loving one's enemies; for then he spoke no longer of human love, but of God's *agape*. God's love for the sinner is the clearest expression for the new relation with God. "The Chris-

[1] This paragraph and the following are a summary of the author's rendering of Nygren's doctrine of *agape* in his book, *Swedish Contributions to Modern Theology*, pp. 108-130.

tian way of fellowship with God depends wholly on the Divine *agape*; thus the question how far those whom God loves deserve His love falls to the ground. To the question, Why does God love? there is only one right answer: Because it is His nature (*essentia*) to love."[2] In succinct sections, Nygren then defines *agape* as spontaneous, unmotivated, value-indifferent, creative love productive of fellowship. *Agape* is entirely, unconditionally independent of the worth of its object. There is no relation whatsoever between *agape* and its object, except the free overflowing of creative love, which by the power of its purity, is productive of the highest fellowship. Nygren sums up his view in unforgettable words: "Hence in this respect also the advent of *agape* implies a complete revolution. Hitherto the possibility of man's fellowship with God has been summed up in the question of what way man could attain unto God. But now, when the way of self-abasement and amendment is set on one side as decisively as the way of righteousness and merit, the conclusion follows that there is no way from

[2] Nygren, *op. cit.*, p. 52.

[72]

man's side by which he can attain unto God. . . . There is no way from man to God other than the way which God has made in coming to man: the way of the divine *agape* and the divine forgiveness. *Agape* is God's own way to man."[3]

Naturally, there is no time here even to intimate Nygren's scholarly comparison of Platonism, Aristotelianism, and Neo-Platonism with Christianity as *agape*, or even to suggest his treatment of the parables of Jesus or the basic unity of the New Testament along with the clash of motifs in it. Particularly important would be a discussion of the *eros* motif from man to God which Nygren analyzes into its most subtle and noble forms of historic expression. In general, *eros* can be defined as man's seeking of his highest good. Wherever the emphasis is on a relationship, however nobly depicted, where a subject chooses a certain course of conduct because of the value of it, because it can improve him, help him to realize his best self, even because he thinks it leads him to God and thus to his highest good, there *eros* is the dominating motif. According to

[3] *Ibid.*, p. 56.

Nygren, Christianity has never been a case of pure *agape*, but always a matter of *agape* in its struggle with the *eros* motif. Instead of completely surrendering to God's love and living in its power, men have tried to help God out, to work out their own salvation in fear and trembling. This is always a matter of *eros*, not of *agape*. Another tendency as seen in the Gospel of John has been to limit *agape* to the love of brethren, or to single out God's love for His Son, which might have definite motivation, or to emphasize the Father's loving the disciples *because* they have loved the Son. In some places, the love of the world is specifically forbidden. All limitations placed on *agape*, however, impair its purity. *Agape* knows of no restrictions. It is unbounded love not dependent upon external conditions. The New Testament, thus, is not claimed to witness exclusively for *agape*; but the new, the distinctive in Christianity is this idea of unmotivated, groundless love. Formally, it is best expressed and at its highest by John: "God is Love"; but as to content, Paul's hymn to love in *I. Corinthians* 13 is by far the best description of it. The parables of Jesus where goodness is practiced out of sheer love, like that of the Prodigal Son, the Good Samaritan, the Laborers in the Vineyard receiving equal reward—express the deepest in Christianity. So do the commandments to love one's enemies, to forgive endlessly, and the declarations of God's indiscriminate shining on the righteous and the unrighteous, and, more, of God's loving the world so that He gave. Since, however, it is natural for man to have self-reference, to seek his highest good, the two motifs *agape* and *eros* struggled along for centuries, perhaps for the most part unconsciously, until that great genius, Augustine, synthesized them into the *caritas* motif. *Agape* meant uncalculating love; *eros* meant man's seeking the highest good. *Caritas* combined them by finding man's highest good in uncalculating love which God alone could give. By his synthesis, however, Augustine broke down the basic purity of the Christian motif: he made the theological lion and lamb of God's grace and man's effort or merit lie down together. He reconciled *amor Dei* with *amor sui*. Nygren himself can best summarize Augustine's

[75]

relation to the *agape* motif: "From the point of view of the object, Augustine's view is emphatically theocentric, in that no object can compete with God for our love, but in the relation to the nature of love it is equally egocentric, for even in God I seek *my* good."[4] This, then, is the Augustinian synthesis of *eros* and *agape* into *caritas*: the universal eudaemonism and man's efforts to satisfy it, i.e. the human reference, are combined with God's way to man *sola gratia* in the Incarnation, while man's self-love is seen to be satisfiable only in his uncalculable love to God. This great synthesis conquered and ruled Catholic thought. It would be interesting to study how Catholic thought made this combination even firmer by its three ladders to God: the *meritum* ladder of moralism, the analogic ladder of speculation, and the anagogic ladder of mysticism; but all we can add here is that Luther tore down Augustine's subtle synthesis and restored and deepened the basic motif of pure Christianity by his insistence on salvation through faith alone, through a faith which is through and

[4] Nygren, *Den kristna kärlekstanken*, Vol. II, p. 357.

through the work of God's grace, a faith which is not a fulfillment of man's deepest nature, since man has nothing at all with which to commend himself in the eyes of God.

In order to determine to what extent we can accept and use this idea in our interpretation, an evaluation of it seems necessary. Of utmost theological importance is Nygren's analysis of motifs establishing *agape* as the distinctive and determinative element in Christianity. Contemporary thought is suffering from a fit of confusion. Having escaped from a narrow and unintelligent dogmatism where the uniqueness of Christianity was taken for granted as an essential aspect of God's only Revelation, Christian thinkers, in many circles, are now all too frequently ready to renounce as prejudice or lack of knowledge the Christian claim to have a distinctive message for the world. Those who still cling to the uniqueness of Christianity have usually either some vague notion of a supernatural variety expressed in a Christology where God revealed Himself as God only once, in the Incarnation, or else some popular idea, seldom critically appraised, to the effect that Christianity is unique because it alone had a founder who fully lived and even died for his religion, that good will first became connected with religion through the life and teachings of Jesus, or that inwardness and spiritual freedom are the contributions exclusively of Christian faith. If only because of the general confusion and vagueness on this topic, the scholarly nature of Nygren's investigation has rendered us much service. His entire historical approach, which we cannot, of course, discuss in this connection, is more adequate as well as more challenging than any other with which the writer is acquainted. By it, in any case, he has opened up broad but rigorous avenues to historical investigation of religion which many a thoughtful scholar is likely to wish patiently to explore.

That *agape* is the determinative and distinctive motif of Christianity seems certain. This does not mean, of course, that it is either the most common idea in Christian doctrine or the most usual motive of Christian action. The investigation does not attempt to be descriptive in a sociological sense. Nygren is careful not to claim that *agape* is the characteristic element in Christianity from the point of view of either the number of believers in it or the quantity of historical doctrine. He himself claims only that it is the basic motif, in the light of which the distinctive genius of Christianity can best be understood. We have stressed, therefore, the notion of a determinative motif, since to some people the idea of distinctiveness would mean nothing more than that difference whereby Christianity can be set apart from all other religions. Nygren is very definite, however, that with "distinctive" is meant not only an additive notion, but also an essential idea without which Christian thought as an historic phenomenon cannot be adequately understood. In this assertion we can wholeheartedly acquiesce. Christianity cannot be completely comprehended except through its distinctive idea of love. There are many ideas which are called love. Christianity is more than a general theory of good will. It is a system of thought and a proposed way of life in which God's love is at the center, necessitating, according to its nature, a fellowship on the part of those who have received it. Reference to this freely given, uncalculating love meets us everywhere in the teachings of Jesus. To say this is not to assert that there are in the Gospels no ideas inadequate to *agape* or inconsistent with it, but it is confidently to affirm that the Christian idea of love is there as both the distinctive and the determinative idea. It seems obvious that we cannot understand the teachings of Jesus apart from such parables as the Prodigal Son, the Good Samaritan, the Laborers in the Vineyard, or apart from such injunctions as the love of enemies, or certainly not apart from a view of God as freely forgiving, as allowing His sun to shine on both the evil and the good. The entire emphasis of Nygren on the unity of the New Testament seen in the light of the Christian idea of love offers much to this old problem. Surely, the Christian idea of love is characteristic of both the Johannine and the Pauline writings, whatever be their points of irreconcilable disagreement. That the Christian idea of love is even developed and made more explicit both formally and practically in Paul and John, Nygren, himself, has pointed out. The writings of Paul and the Johannine literature go beyond this, moreover, for they also begin to interpret the life of Jesus, himself, in terms of the operation of the divine Love. The Christian Church has ever since continued this interpretation of Jesus as a part of the original Source of this *agape*. In so doing it has often, to be sure, become imaginative and even magical; but its fundamental insight has been unerring, namely that heavenly light came through a historic life, and that this life must itself somehow be connected with the Source of that light. In any case, Christian thought as a whole and at its deepest cannot be satisfactorily understood, in spite of all directly contrary doctrines and practices, except in terms of *agape* as its explanatory motif. The essence of the Christian Revelation is that somehow there came into historical awareness in the person of Jesus an understanding of God and His relation with men which is unique in the history of the world. The basic idea contained in this understanding is that God is Love, willing to give Himself for sinful men, to suffer with them, and to save them into a fellowship based not on man's merit, but on forgiving love.

Be this idea accepted or rejected, the emphasis placed on it by Nygren as simply a historic truth is vitally needed.

Whether or not the notion of *agape* is to be found in any pre-Christian literature, or in any writings not directly dependent on Christian sources, is another question. The writer, in any case, is not aware of any non-Christian literature where the full idea of God's *agape* appears. Stoicism's universal love of mankind is both too immanentistic and too pantheistic to be on the same personal level as Christian *agape*, while it is also far too much a matter of living according to reason and natural law to be totally uncalculating. Buddhism's use of "good will toward all the world," on the other hand, is too negative to be *agape*, the reference being not to active goodness freely giving itself, and solely concerned with the good of its object, but being, rather, the quiet cutting off of all enmity and evil desire for the sake of harmony and spiritual invulnerability. A much nearer idea is that implied by the supposed action of the Buddha when, upon his becoming enlightened, he denied himself the supreme privilege of entering into nirvana simply out of compassion for his fellow sufferers, that he might preach to them deliverance from evil, or better, perhaps, that he might teach those willing and able to understand the truth which alone can free them from their terrifying illusions. This idea did not, however, become the central principle of explanation in Buddhism, but remained an exceptional instance which really contradicted its inner spirit and meaning. The idea that reality at its very core is redemptive love, and that men to be saved must have this as the God-given source of their conduct, was definitely not a part of Oriental religions prior to their contact with Christian doctrines. The problem of the Bhakti sects in Hinduism is too complicated to discuss in this short survey; but they are, in any case, post-Christian and may even be due to Christian influence. The full doctrine of Christian *agape* is, furthermore, and not to overstate the case, not the essential element in the Bhakti approach. It is, far rather, a very emotional form of the *eros* motif. The Chinese idea of *jen*, or mutual benevolence, seems to fall short of the Christian idea of love by its conception of mutuality. More important still, of course, is the fact that it is an ethical rule rather than a religious assertion as to ultimate reality. According to critical scholars and in the light of the total meaning of Taoism, in Lao-tse's famous sentence, "Recompense injury with *teh*," *teh* is not rightly translated by kindness; and Confucius' negative statement of the Golden Rule is hedged in by an express prohibition of meeting evil with kindness. Both Lao-tse's Taoism with its negative ontology and its passive ethics and Confucius' stress on the human source of morality preclude their meaningful comparison to the Christian idea of love.

That the Old Testament has passages which approach the idea of *agape*, to be sure, Nygren freely admits. The great chapter in *Deutero-Isaiah* describing the Suffering Servant is, however, more of an explanation of what seemed unjust punishment and a propounding of the value of vicarious suffering than the full idea of God's indiscriminate love as the deepest interpretation of reality and as the highest rule for human conduct. Except for its particularity of reference, a certain passage in *Hosea* (11:9) comes close to the idea of *agape*: "I will not execute the fierceness of mine anger, I will not return to destroy Ephraim: for I am God, and not man." The correctness of the passage or the authorship makes no difference in this case, since it can surely be established that the verses are pre-Christian. Even if the idea of the great invitation in *Isaiah* 1:18 should originally have been negative rather than positive, this, too, is irrelevant inasmuch as this textual change also is without a doubt pre-Christian. The passage as it stands sounds very much like *agape*: "Though your sins be as scarlet, they shall be as white as snow; though they be red like crimson, they shall be as wool." The fact that this version of it is very likely a sentimental misreading or change of the original and that it is found in a context where *agape* is entirely out of place, would make us very hesitant to count the passage as an indication of a full view of God, of His relation with men, and of men's ideal fellowship with each other. The psalmist's tender pronouncement, "like as a father pitieth his children" (*Psalm* 103:13) may,

[85]

to be sure, in one breath stress the unworthiness of the object, but in the next, restrict the father's pity to those who fear him. According to recognized Jewish scholars, the Jewish apocryphal literature has statements about love, beyond that of love to God and neighbor, that approach the statements made by Jesus; but they seem not to treat love as the deepest reality in the universe and as the final standard of conduct. In Jewish apocryphal literature either the Law or Wisdom is the regulative norm as far as God's relation with the world is concerned. The Jewish pronouncement regarding love to God and to neighbor, although indicative of a strong stress on the idea of love, and although exceedingly prominent in pre-Christian Jewish thought, is, nevertheless, too much on the line from man to God and includes too much of the idea of calculation to be *agape*. Judaism has ethical precepts of going beyond the measure, of having a yielding, forgiving disposition, and this has some reflection in its view of God, but the writer has not found in Jewish literature the completely Christian idea of love. Indeed, although the writer does not claim expert knowledge of the history of religions, he has, at least, never come across in his readings in the field a complete statement of *agape* in any non-Christian literature. Plato's tender mention of God as the shepherd of mankind seems, like Stoicism's ideas of the World-Soul, to be nearly hid behind the stress on His reasonableness, and fails of that groundlessness characteristic of the Christian idea of love, of that unmotivated giving of itself, solely because it is its nature to give. Outside Christianity, then, although there are certain ideas similar to that of the Christian idea of love, the resemblances are largely superficial. We can say, therefore, with some confidence, that *agape* is not only the determinative but also the distinctive motif of the Christian religion. God's revelation in Christ must be understood in terms of the Christian idea of love as expressive of the deepest truth in the universe and as the highest ethical standard for mankind.

When all this has been said, however, there are a few fundamental problems connected with Nygren's definition of Christianity as *agape* that must claim our attention. If we grant that *agape*

[87]

as the Christian idea of love is the basic motif of Christianity, we must be careful before accepting Nygren's full description of it. His central idea of it, for instance, is that it is exclusively God's way to man. It is, naturally, of utmost importance to understand that the religion of Jesus was centered in God: it was God, not man, who was to bring in the Kingdom; we should be perfect even as our Heavenly Father is perfect. This fact, however, should not blind us to the great part that humanism played in the thought and teachings of Jesus. Both in method and in substance of teaching, Jesus made much use of the natural and human realm, arguing directly from them to God. On this point we need not be afraid of "the peril of modernizing Jesus." The point is too obvious even to need demonstration. The power and relevance of Jesus' teachings are due primarily to the fact that he extracted the best in human relationships, applying this both to the supernatural realm and to the common ways of human life. The exceptional became the ultimately real and the rule for the commonplace. If even an earthly father can rise above the customary spirit and demands of the law and, by the power of his love, restore his erring son, how much more must God freely forgive those who seek Him. If the shepherd for the sake of a lost sheep is willing to leave the ninety-and-nine, if he values the one sheep so highly, how much more joy will there be in heaven when a child of God's creation turns again home. If the master of a vineyard can take pity on those who have worked but an hour, how much more will God deal with those who serve Him, not after their desert, but after His goodness. "If ye then, being evil, know how to give good gifts unto your children, how much more shall your Father which is in heaven. . . ." If even an earthly judge, for the sake of his own convenience, will give heed to the pleadings of an importunate widow, how much more will God, who is Love, be anxious to help those in distress who continue to seek His aid. The body of Jesus' teachings, moreover, seems shot through and through with worldly wisdom and practical advice. Those who wish to be saved must not be like the foolish virgins who did not plan ahead. Spontaneous goodness is not enough. Wisdom is also needed, even the wisdom of serpents. In spiritual warfare man ought to count the cost as much as the King who plans a campaign. There is even a question as to whether Jesus did not hold as the ultimate sanction of right action not the Sadducees' right for its own sake, nor the Pharisees' right for the love of God, but the Essenes' right for the sake of future reward in heaven. This point is at least debatable. Perhaps Jesus' double stress on inwardness and on future reward was the secret of his power with people who could not fully understand the depths of his instruction. Even the disciples seem to have been motivated by a desire for reward in the Kingdom, and to have been promised it as well. Then, too, Jesus undoubtedly did emphasize the value of the individual: Ye are of so much value that "even the very hairs of your head are all numbered"; "What shall a man give in exchange for his soul?" Jesus even spoke of being "rich toward God," of laying up "a treasure in the heavens that faileth not." There are instances in his teachings where even expediency on a very human plane plays a large role. To go into this problem, however, is

[90]

unnecessary, for Nygren's attempt to interpret Jesus' teaching of *agape* as a totally unnatural, divine gift exclusively from God to man does not square easily with the New Testament. The philosophical and ethical objections to it which naturally arise are another question. In this instance, Nygren's reliance on a modern mood, not without Barthian coloring, which finds more response in the teachings of Paul than in those of Jesus, seems to have made less acceptable his doctrine of *agape*.

The notion that the Christian idea of love is entirely from God to man also makes for an artificial Christology which tends to remove Jesus from man. At the center of this dualism between God and man lies a substance philosophy where personality is not the ultimate of ontology. Gilson has pointed out what harm and confusion come from not making Being in personal terms ontologically ultimate. The full significance of this philosophical insight, however, is seldom applied to theology. We naturally agree that God's *agape* was revealed in Jesus because God took the initiative, because God entered actively into history; but we cannot separate Jesus from the solidarity of mankind. We cannot give him an artificial manhood. In a recent discussion, a disciple of Nygren, when pressed by the author, declared that Sabellianism was really no heresy; that the Trinity can be explained chronologically rather that analytically; that God the Father came down and became God the Son. Although this view may not be representative of Nygren's view as a whole, nevertheless, it is indicative of a tendency wherein God's *agape* is somehow limited, in a special way quite beyond explanation, to the Incarnation. We can agree with Nygren that in the life and death of Jesus we see the majesty of God as the "sacrificial, self-giving majesty of love." We must, however, remain content with the historic doctrine that Jesus was both God and man, that God was in him, that the importance of Jesus is, first of all, that God was seen in him, but in a fully historic, human personality.

It is unfortunate, indeed, that Nygren's view of philosophy precludes the rational evaluation of theological theory and the subsequent exclusion of whatever themes are inconsistent with

its basic motif. Either his methodological limitation of theology to the description of the historical content of Christianity has made it necessary
for him to include as Christian a great number
of thoughts inadequate to or inconsistent with
agape, or else the desire to keep intact traditional
theology has helped not a little to fashion his
theological method. Nygren, for instance, will
maintain with great vigor that only that which
can be explained in terms of the *agape* motif is
Christian; but when confronted with notions
such as eternal hell or other traditionalistic dogmas, totally at variance with the Christian idea
of love, he will counter with the assertion that
all we know about *agape* is to be found in the
history of Christian thought. No rational criticism of such aspects of traditional theology
which go contrary to the notion of *agape* is allowed, on the ground that *agape* is not a human
love and cannot be understood in terms of human
thought. In this way, to use a popular expression,
Nygren manages to have his cake and eat it, too.
He can be both a liberal stressing God's love as
basic to Christianity, and, at the same time, he

can, as far as he lets himself, be a theological reactionary, accepting those very ideas which, humanly speaking, go contrary to the Christian idea of love. This alliance of the Christian idea of love with those ideas of traditional theology inconsistent with it seems like an impossible straddling of the fence, a dangerous and destructive halting on both sides. Philosophical and theological criticism cannot permanently be evaded merely by calling the content of faith alogical, paradoxical, or religion's own answer to its own questions. It is easy to see that the idea of *agape* and much in traditional theology clash with all violence. *Agape* as faith's final principle of explanation is an idea of ultimate hope and historic challenge; whereas traditional theology maintains a split universe, an unsolvable dualism, an eternal heaven and an eternal hell. The traditional view of God is also anything but that of God as *agape*; whatever love it has is buried under doctrines and beliefs which smother it by their very contradictions of it. The resolute acceptance of the Christian idea of love and its application to all the spheres of theology would result in a system of

[94]

thought where everything is ultimately subject to God's love. Whatever be the many inadequacies of liberalism, its stress on God as victorious love must be maintained.

This inconsistency Nygren maintains by confining himself to the nature of God and to His work as a Redeemer. He fails to connect God the Redeemer with God the Creator. Somehow, God, if He is all-good, all-powerful, and all-wise, is responsible for the world that He has made and for the children of His creation. It is easy, of course, to say that we must not measure God by the measure of man, but must He not be better, at least, than our best measure of Him?

The doctrine of God cannot be isolated from that of the world. Nygren has said little about the wisdom and the power of God. Although faith is supposed to hold that He is both all-wise and all-powerful, the point remains that either God is the Creator of this world, who knew what He was doing, and who will, in His own way, accomplish a completely good end, or else He is in some way limited. No matter what the nature of that limitation might be, if

God is to be thought of as a sufficiently wise and powerful, completely good Will, the choice between a limited God and, ultimately somehow, a universal salvation stands. On this point every theologian must make up his mind. There has been too much equivocation on or outright evasion of this problem for Christian theology to be interpretatively adequate. To place the problem beyond the limits of faith is not satisfactory unless all ultimate questions are placed there, too. The proposition that God is perfect in every respect involves definite implications. God's ultimate victory, the identification of God the Creator with God the Redeemer and with God the Conqueror of evil, is, of course, a bold venture of faith. Surely it cannot be arrived at through a rational interpretation of actuality. Yet we dare to think that the need of Christian theology is to live not by despair, but by hope; not by fear, but by faith. Only when the Christian idea of love is applied not only to redemption, but to creation and eschatology as well, can Christian theology feed on the faith which is the conviction of things not seen. It seems that the choice between such a baffling faith and a limited God offers the only alternatives for Christian theology.

In one place, Nygren points out that *agape* must exist in a constant tension with *nomos* or law. Undoubtedly, *agape* can never come into the fullness of its power as a principle of interpretation until it is organically related to both law and reason. *Nomos* involves those traditional norms which help to direct present experience. They are necessary aspects of historic development and personal growth. *Nomos* must ever be in the service of *agape*. Tension between the two, although likely, is, however, not necessary. Tension results only when means to life become its ends. This frequently happens in the case of moral and spiritual laws, wherein the keeping of laws itself becomes an objective. The reason for the law or the historic circumstances that brought it into being are not understood. Men begin to exist for the Sabbath when the Sabbath should exist for men. Religious practices or doctrines are maintained as sacred long after their function has passed, and even when they work hardship on

[97]

the people they were designed to help. Personal relationships are hemmed in by man's own legal creations; the past suppresses and impedes abundance of life. In this case, *nomos* has become an end, and, being no longer in the service of *agape*, is evil. It is not this fact, however, that Nygren considers, but, rather, that the works of the law can become a way to God. Men may believe that by the keeping of the law they can earn their salvation. This is, of course, an altogether natural belief, since obedience and service are highly valued in family life and in social life as a whole. We hope, too, that right doing is acceptable service in the sight of the Lord. Anti-nomianism constitutes a real spiritual danger. If God seeks man's love, however, and desires him to love his neighbor, man cannot naturally, reach God simply by means of the works of the law. The father and the mother want more of their children than obedience and service; they want their love, their trust, and their fellowship. In the same way, the law cannot lead men to God, and fear of it often hides for them God's face. Or, on the other hand, if a person takes pride in the keeping of the law

[98]

so that he is thereby hindered from knowing his own sins and failures and from knowing God more fully and serving Him more humbly, then the keeping of the law can definitely separate man from God. Naturally, too, there is a tension between man's sense of independence, his wishing to earn his salvation, and the necessity of recognizing the primacy of God's grace and the reception of it with humble gratitude. When all this is said, however, the relation of *agape* and *nomos* brings up one of the basic inconsistencies in Nygren's thought: his insistence that God's fellowship with man is on the basis not of God's holiness, but of man's sinfulness. In Roman Catholic thought, it is held, the attempt is to lift men up to God to have fellowship with Him upon the basis of His holiness, whereas in Protestant thought, especially that of Luther, the insistence is that man's fellowship with God is ever on the basis of man's sinfulness. The whole question, however, is falsely presented. Man's relationship with God is neither on the basis of holiness nor on the basis of sinfulness, since both are legal thoughts, but on the basis of God's love, the relation of a Father to his needy, misunderstanding, wayward children. The relation of parents with their children in an ideal family relationship is not primarily on the basis of good or evil, but on the basis of tender affection. The Prodigal Son came home and was received into the father's arms neither on the basis of sin nor of holiness, but simply on the basis of love and of sonship. Nygren, on the other hand, would keep the son a servant. Although the forgiveness would be complete, there would nevertheless be a constant cleft between him and his father. The legalism which offers a choice between sin and holiness as the basis of man's relationship with God is surely entirely inconsistent with the basicness of the Christian idea of love.

Naturally, the Christian idea of love must be related to the function of reason in religion. When asked why his system seemingly had to give such an appearance of being a reactionary irrationalism, Nygren frankly replied that as yet time has not permitted him to work out the relation of love to reason. Since the question is still open, our best procedure is to wait for a fuller

and more final answer. The insistence that it is
not rational for a holy God to stoop to save sinners is, of course, ill-founded. If God is love, the
most natural thing imaginable is that by His very
nature He should desire to save the children of
His creation. It is enough to say in this connection that religion is not reasonable if with a reasoned religion is meant the production of religious
dogmas through rational speculation according
to the inherent powers of the mind; for religion
is through and through a matter of revelation, of
faith's believing its ideals obtained from experience to be objectively real, beyond man's experience. If, on the other hand, with reasonableness
is meant that religion is not revealed apart from
the function of reason in its interpreting and testing of experience, then we hold religion to be
without a question reasonable. The decision of
faith or the moral decision may at the moment of
choice lie deeper than immediate rational review,
but it is ever and ever dependent upon the previous experience, at least in part rationally interpreted, of itself and of the whole race. Revealed
religion can never be a direct contradiction of

[101]

reasoned truth. Vital religion is, rather, the progressive synthesis of the ideal and the actual by both thought and deed.

This brings up our main problem. To be meaningful as the distinctive and determinative motif of Christianity, provided that faith holds Christianity to be universally adequate and applicable, *agape* must in some way be organically related to the whole of man, the whole of history, and the whole of nature. It would, however, be unfair to expect this of Nygren, inasmuch as his chosen task is not synthesis but analysis. Nygren himself has stressed the fact that certain epochs of thought are synthetic in spirit, while others need the discipline of diastase. With widening horizons, Christian thought came close to being interpreted entirely in terms of Old Testament derivations, New Testament surroundings, and general cultural conditions through which it has passed, without any consciousness that it had a unique message, that as a religion it was decidedly distinctive. Then, too, not only was Christianity in danger of losing its identity because of a confused historical method, neither sufficiently critical nor rich in analytical insight, but also it was threatened by a vague rationalistic method, working from the generalities of experience without appreciation of the necessity of faith's choice among the historic traditions which through unusual personalities and historic communities have given certain answers to the problems of life reaching beyond any general theory that is dependent entirely on the rational description of actuality. In this way, revelation succumbed to reason, and theology became equated with the philosophy of religion. Reason can never by itself, however, working solely with average experience and without the compulsive power of faith, leap to the ideal which provides religion with social and personal adequacy. The ontological argument is primarily not rational but religious in nature. Every religion is conditioned by the will to believe, but the intent of this will is not, first of all, to obtain comforting or even helpful illusions in order that they might become effective reals, but, much rather, to discover an objective truth that will sustain and make available the ideal which at times gleams like an unattainable star beyond the horizon of the actual. Religion in this sense is not man-made but God-made. Man can believe with religious power and devotion only as long as what he believes is more than his own creation. Religions are historic developments, not rational creations. Faith, to be adequate, must find its sum and substance in a historic religion.

Nygren has certainly performed an invaluable service by calling attention to the fact that the vague thinking of today, where religions are interpreted solely in terms of some general moral development, some common cultural conditions, or some broad, rational speculations, must give way to the critical analysis of a new day, where the distinctive point of view of each religion is recognized as faith's attempt to answer, not formal considerations, but the absolute questions of life. Nygren has said not that synthesis is wrong, but, rather, that it has its place. His point is, therefore, well taken that his task must first of all be a critical discovery of the basic motif of Christianity. This task represents a most important theological contribution. Careful analysis ought always to precede important synthesis. We must know what Christianity has to say about human motives before we can relate its demands to the whole man; what it has to say about the relationship of God and man before we can relate it to other religions; what it has to say about God's relation with the whole world before we can relate it to a rational interpretation of nature. We differ with Nygren, however, in our position that reason can compare motifs, and that it can relate these both to philosophic problems and to psychological data. If God has created us, the *eros* in our nature must somehow be related to the *agape* which should form the source of our conduct. In man himself, God's work as Creator and Redeemer must be reconciled. Hocking discusses the sublimation of instincts in the remaking of human nature, while A. A. Bowman takes issue with him in this respect, believing that a total transformation of man's distinctive drives is somehow necessary. The point is, however, that whether we have sublimation, transformation, or even destruction and substitution of natural drives, those drives have, in their way, fulfilled an important function in the development of God's creative plan. Only today's good can judge yesterday's evil; only tomorrow's better can judge today's good; only the ideal can judge the actual. Whether the actual serves as a way to the ideal, a necessary stage before it can come, or even as a contrast for it, the higher development, nevertheless, has no right to refuse to see its relation to it. Still, the ideal must inevitably, by its very nature, condemn the actual, for it seeks eternally its own concretion. If God is to be both Creator and Redeemer, and if man must be understood as experiencing both *agape* and *eros*, some one must work out the relation between them. For this reason, we must think highly of Augustine's synthesis of *agape* and *eros* into *caritas*, for here *eros* is in the service of God's *agape*. *Eros* finds its fulfillment in incalculable love to God. We do not think that Augustine meant that love of God is consistent with man's highest selfishness, but, rather, that man's natural self-centered drive for satisfaction can find its release only in that love of God and neighbor for which it is meant. When man finds this love, he is delivered from his selfish drive for satisfaction by the finding of a satisfaction in God which so completely fulfils his inner cravings that his love of God and men takes the place of his selfishness. The reconciliation of *amor Dei* and *amor sui* seems merely the restatement of Jesus' assertion that only by losing our lives can we find them. We believe that Augustine taught that by loving God man finds his highest happiness, but this kind of happiness is that fulfillment of it which is also the destruction of his selfishness. We think that Augustine would say with Niebuhr that "self-love is never justified, but self-realization is allowed as the unintended but inevitable consequence of unselfish action."[5] In any case, when the analytical task of theology is done, the synthetical must begin, and *agape* and *eros* must again be synthesized into at least a genetic relationship. The writer believes that a coordinate relationship also exists between the two motifs, and that this is the reason for man's being torn between the ideal and the actual, between selfish drives and the sincere desire to

[5] Reinhold Niebuhr, *An Interpretation of Christian Ethics*, p. 53.

overcome them. In that case, *agape* would come not entirely as a sudden gift, nor as a total relationship, but would have its beginning and development in man's gradual growth under the constraint of God's Holy Spirit.

In the same way, Christianity as *agape* must be related to the other religions of history. If we take the fellowship through God's *agape* to be the highest form of fellowship, then Christianity surely has a distinct message to all other religions. Since this message declares a certain kind of fellowship, it must inevitably be proclaimed both in practice and in theory. It is for this reason that missions must be a matter both of evangelism and of service. Evangelism without service is the practical denial of the inner message of Christian theology. Christian theology without social service is the preaching of a form lacking in meaningfulness apart from the practicing of its content. To this extent we agree with Nygren that religion is more than reasoned truth. By the very nature of *agape*, moreover, the works of Christian love must inevitably overflow into the whole world, quite without regard to its acceptance or

[108]

rejection. When this is said, however, it must also be emphasized that Christianity has an intellectual content of such a general nature that it can be universally applied. Then, too, important victories are first won in the ideal, which only gradually becomes embodied. Nor does Christianity as an ideal, any more than Christ, come to destroy, but to fulfill. The struggle between faiths, contrary to Nygren's assertion, is not a struggle to death. Whatever in the different religions of the world is good, promotive of a higher form of fellowship, whatever ennobles and helps life, must be kept and used in the service of Christ. Christianity is, however, a Gospel with a definite message condemning whatever ignorance, thoughtlessness, or hardness of heart separates God and men, and men and men. Christianity must deny as wrong whatever springs from selfish motives, whatever results from fear, whatever oppresses man with ultimate despair. Sometimes doctrines must be challenged; sometimes practices must be condemned; in neither case, however, because they are not Christian in a sociological sense, but because they are destructive of the highest and best fellowship in the place where it is believed and practiced. The great thing about the Christian idea of love is that it is wide enough to include all forms of fellowship, every kind of communal life. All forms of fellowship can be changed with *agape* as their source and standard.[6] Christianity as the belief in the ultimate victory of a two-dimensional fellowship based on *agape* must, therefore, be effectively related to every kind of fellowship this world has to offer.

[6] A concrete confrontation of the Christian fellowship with a non-Christian fellowship will be undertaken in Chapter VII.

IV

Liberal Thought and the Religious Absolute

LIBERALISM as a religious movement seems to have failed. This is currently the verdict of history. Before the tribunal of time, liberalism as a fundamental attitude of life has been declared wanting. Only recently has the seriousness of the religious situation seeped deeply into our American consciousness, and we are just now becoming aware that this desperateness is not so much post-war as post-Protestant, that is, a protest with not a few decades, but a few centuries for a background.

Recently an ardent liberal suggested that liberalism has failed because we liberals have failed to be evangelical. But can liberalism be evangelical? Are not the two terms inevitably contradictory? Is not liberalism by its very nature negative in method and result? History gives significant suggestions even if no final answers.

Historically, liberalism arose as a reaction against a certain kind of supernaturalism represented by the Roman Catholic Church which impeded progress by its refusal of free thought. This institutionalized supernaturalism demanded that all thought and values conform to its standards. In order to achieve scientific progress, however, truth had to be defined in terms of man's reason and tested experience. By means of this standard for scientific truth such notable results were effected that it was only natural for reason and testable experience to become the criteria of true knowledge in every sphere of man's thought. In this light, it is definitely a mistake to call the big revolution in thought that of the nineteenth century, for then merely came to fruition previously existing tendencies which underlie both Protestantism and liberalism. That thesis is fundamentally sound which claims that we are entering a new epoch of thought, for in both the philosophical and the theological fields the deepest presuppositions of the past are being weighed, and, in many instances, found wanting. A deep reaction against the old supernaturalism which lacked capacity for the fullest freedom is coming to its culmination; and not without prophetic insight are some thinkers even speaking of the post-Protestant period of religious history. Perhaps the present movement is towards a new catholicity which will accept a different form of supernaturalism and amply allow for the most cherished values of liberalism.

The liberalism which has been ripening during the last few centuries was based on an attitude of trust in the inherent capacities of man, whether to control nature, to solve his social problems, or to understand the nature of the reality which he experiences. With the birth of commerce, with the rise of cities and nations, with the development of technique and the growth of science, with world discoveries and widening horizons, with the incoming of "the subjectivist bias" in philosophy and the growth of empiricism, with the industrial revolution, with the birth of the historical and the social sciences—with all these and with all similar phenomena the growth of liberalism as an historical movement is inseparably connected. Scientific technique, the empirical stress in philosophy, individualism in social and political theory—these truly are of the essence of liberalism.

The revolt against an inadequate supernaturalism gave man greater freedom, fuller truth, more tangible values. To worst the oppressor the method of doubt with its demand for demonstrability was soon placed in the saddle. Demonstrability, moreover, was at first interpreted both rationally and empirically, that is, in terms of both clear and distinct ideas and applicability to facts; but with the fading of belief in the supernatural and with a growing man-centeredness of thought, the sphere of accepted truth was soon reduced to those aspects in experience which could be tested by logic or by scientific experiment. The attitude which accompanied the method of doubt, furthermore, settled into a mood deeper than conscious thought, and soon began to question the reality of anything supernatural.

This freedom from supernaturalism was won by two sharp weapons: history and reason. History as a science destroyed, for those who heeded

it, the old supernaturalism by means of its critical
scholarship. The most cherished claims of supernaturalism became definitely suspect, and in many
cases proved invalid. Biblical literalism was given
up in thoughtful circles, but very slowly and re-
luctantly. When this had to be done, the great
Ritschl meant to captivate the stronghold of the
enemy by using its own weapons, by making the
historical Jesus the unique revelation of God; but
this doctrine acted as a boomerang by occasion-
ing an astounding interest in the life of Jesus, an
interest which eventuated in the radical scholarship of recent years! In short, and merely to suggest a line of thought, liberalism's use of history
not only destroyed a literalistic supernaturalism,
claiming uniqueness and absoluteness, but threatened historic Christianity and, in truth, religion
as a whole, by the unavoidable problem of his-
toricism or relativism. The study of the history
of religions with its genetic approach, moreover,
tracing the origin of the Christian motifs or com-
paring them with those of non-Christian religions
had the same effect; the freedom that liberalism
sought from supernaturalism resulted not a little

in relativism, and in many quarters in agnosticism, whether uttered or unexpressed.

Similarly, the use of reason and the stress on man's experience as the criteria for truth made for a certain light and freedom, but at what cost? No matter what religious systems of thought were now framed, the problem of illusionism haunted them all. With an undue emphasis on the problem of knowledge, a man-centered problem, "the egocentric predicament" strongly challenged religious belief; and since faith as a medium of knowledge became all too often a mere adjunct to reason, man's fundamental religious attitude could not escape that most serious temptation, agnosticism. With the growth of psychology, furthermore, with its ideas of rationalization and sublimation, psychologism or subjectivism settled as an impenetrable cloud over many earnest religious thinkers, a cloud which, despite their attempts, they could not too successfully smile away by their half-understood theories of practical reason. Thus did man use reason to gain his freedom from supernaturalism; but in so doing, he inflicted a most serious wound on himself. His joy in freedom has been smothered in his uncertainty as to what to do with it, and his values have lost meaningfulness by their being considered relative, or, at least, not definitely known as objectively real. This change within liberalism is the disillusionment that we are now experiencing. Liberalism has changed from a negative evangelicalism demanding freedom into an apology for the possession of that freedom.

This struggle for freedom through fuller light was, moreover, one of the distinct dangers of liberalism. The Socratic identification of the good with knowledge stole even into Christian thought. Redemption became a term often less meaningful than religious education, while the latter became considered, consciously or unconsciously, a main road to salvation. The thoroughly moralistic thought "salvation through character" became in many circles substituted for the fullness of the religious content. The way to achieve character, furthermore, was through a religious education which was neither true education nor religion. Man, it was assumed, was naturally good, and if exposed to fullness of ex-

[117]

perience, man would, in the long run, make the right choices. Because of this false identification of the good with knowledge, liberalism resolutely rejected any form of rigid indoctrination, and refused to guide the social and the individual experience by any form of dogma. Due to this mistaken notion, moreover, a liberal view of education in circles where liberalism was dominating thought, came to take the place of creedal indoctrination, of catechetical instruction, and of emotional evangelicalism. At a recent meeting of outstanding liberal leaders, editors, publishers, professors, and ministers, reference was continually made to experience as the final criterion of truth, without seemingly any consciousness of the color experience has received through the ages, or of the complex relation between previous belief and the nature of the experience itself and its subsequent interpretation. Liberalism has usually worked with a superficial theory of knowledge, but even more it has failed to distinguish knowledge as such from the deeper realms of religious decision. There is a relation, of course, between love and light, but surely not

[118]

the Socratic identification of virtue and knowledge.

Liberalism's faith in education was but one of its aspects. It had, furthermore, an optimism, religious in some devout circles, but usually a part of the general faith in man as such, an optimism about man, nature, and history. Its attitude towards development both in the individual and in society, insofar as it lacked religious faith and demanded religious standards, was unrealistic. The evolutionary optimism of yesterday has inevitably given way to the defeatism of to-day. Liberalism failed sufficiently to take into account the evil will in man and the evil will in society. There is an evil in man, which, as Professor Winfred Donovan recently declared, seems to have to break out in periods of collective hate and destructiveness. Reinhold Niebuhr's thesis has much foundation in fact, for individually we are held by our social conventions, but when responsibility is divided, even the most moral of us at times gives way to a kind of evil which we as individuals would never dream of committing. Modern psychology also throws a great deal of light on our hidden natures. Liberalism failed sufficiently deeply to relate these incontrovertible facts to its theological interpretations, but history did not fail to notice its significant omissions.

This, then, is our contention: Liberalism arose as man's demand for freedom. In gaining it, liberalism found that it had not the emotional power nor the depth of insight to make use of it for the very reason that as an historic movement it was man-centered, whereas social history needs to be centered in religion. To have lastingly effective social relations, man needs God. The world cannot sustain the burden of its heart without an adequate religion. For this reason, the world has accepted idols; it is dancing wildly, unhappily, and dangerously before the golden calf of man-made absolutisms. The world is made for God, and without Him it encounters ever new forms of disaster. Without the worship of God, the world must find absolutes: in the political-economic realm, totalitarianism; in the religious realm, the new orthodoxy. Our chief concern is this: Will our new orthodoxy be both adequately supernatural and adequately liberal?

Suppose, now, that we liberals renounce the historic form of our liberalism. Suppose that we do admit that we cannot be both liberal in the historic sense and at the same time adequately evangelical. Suppose that we accept as true the idea that liberalism is religiously dangerous because of its negative view of freedom, its lack of psychological power due to its doctrine of doubt, its dearth of compelling convictions. Suppose that we should admit that historic liberalism is at inmost the idolatry of man, that it does not take into consideration what Kant called the radical evil in man, that it has no feeling for the theological doctrine of "a fallen nature." Suppose that we conclude that liberalism is doomed by the discoveries of some modern psychologies as to the essentially evil nature of man, his will to power, his complexes and compensations, his rationalizings and sublimations. Suppose that we even admit that much of our liberalism at bottom has been, whether displayed or concealed, a religious agnosticism rejecting the necessity of an abundant faith in the moral and spiritual supervision of God. *What then?*

What can then constitute for us an object for absolute emotional commitment and still preserve for us those values in liberalism which we cannot honestly relinquish? American fundamentalism is based upon a literalism which definitely we cannot accept. We are yet too liberal at heart to subscribe to a religious fanaticism which has no regard for historical fact and which eventuates in an increasing number of sects in accordance with what facts are deemed the most fundamental. The social gospel, moreover, seems no object demanding our absolute committal unless we have an absolute Gospel. We are not convinced that any "ism" has the final word in the social scene. In the social realm, furthermore, completeness of conviction to the absolute point would, if practiced, lead to swords raised against swords. Absolutism without liberalism is utterly impossible in the political or in the socio-economic realm. In life on this plane there has to be a certain amount of live and let live. The same is true of church-ism, whether in terms of church union, sacramentalism, or ritualism. Without an Absolute behind these ideas, we cannot give our absolute allegiance to it; and if we should, since we cannot agree on the forms, fanaticism would ensue. Yet why not Barthianism? The Continental theology has no false view of man; it has no literalistic doctrine; it has, besides, an eternal absolute. Why not, indeed? Barthianism stresses the power of God at the expense of His love far and away too strongly for us to commit ourselves fully to it. To us, Barthianism may be prophetic, but it is not in the highest sense Christian. There is a determinism in it, which, even if we grant that man's efforts ought not to be included in a theological discussion dealing with his justification, nevertheless leaves a concept of God which goes contrary to our highest conceptions of both love and justice. Even if Barth is himself indefinite on the point of determinism (to the author's knowledge, he has never repudiated certain definite statements to that effect) and even if he put the problem beyond the limits of Christian faith, his doctrine of man, nevertheless, besides being much of an arbitrary, theological abstraction, contains no elements which would in the last analysis give us a higher doctrine of God. Barth plainly will not face this issue, since it involves human standards. We of the liberal tradition are still too empirical in attitude, however, to define love in terms of a historical revelation which can make love punish eternally the children of its own creation. God's love to us must at least be as good as the best love we know, and, we believe, much better. Punishment, hell, must be the decree of God's love, but it must be purposive, not punitive, in nature. If the Christian love be sufficiently strong and wise, heaven can be heaven only when it has emptied hell. Only a failure of nerve and a sense of moral defeatism could make us accept Barthianism as a theological absolute.

The contention may surprise some that the creeds of the Church contain, especially in their Christologies, the deepest truths of the Christian faith, but only of course, if and as the living truth breaks through the man-made forms. Rightly interpreted, the Utrecht formula may, after all, have the solution we are seeking. The author believes that we can accept that statement and still remain positively liberal and unreservedly evangelical. How is this possible? The fundamentalism of evangelical faith must ever need liberalism. We must combine theologically the absolutes of Christian faith with the relativities of the human reason. Since there is much fundamentalism that is destructively illiberal and much liberalism that fails to be fundamental, we must necessarily combine the two. We must be both religiously evangelical and intellectually liberal. In this respect Kant is right, too: "We can, for we must."

Perhaps the problem ought to be more definitely stated before a solution is offered. There are two great traditions in the Western world: the Hebrew and the Greek. The Hebrew is stern and straight, stressing righteousness. Its faith is that of a moralist, although God is ever close in devotion wherever He is worshipped. Its view of God tends towards transcendence. Its ethics is rigorous. Its history is, to a great extent, that of Christian asceticism, and its creed the mortification of the flesh. Calvinism can be understood only as Hebraic in attitude. Puritanism and Prohibition are symbolic of the Hebrew spirit in American life. There is, on the other hand, the Greek attitude desiring fullness of life, aesthetic enjoyment, freedom of expression. The Renaissance and the Romantic Period are historical examples of this spirit. Liberalism is in the main the embodiment in religion of the Greek spirit, seeking the abundant life and easily and happily accepting contacts with other forms of religious thought. Much in the modern prophetic spirit of Continental theology, on the other hand, has in it the rigorous ring of Hebrew exclusiveness. The ascetic spirit dreads pleasures as wrong; the aesthetic seeks fullness of emotional satisfaction. The ascetic spirit emphasizes right conduct, and thus often leads to the excesses of an unhappy holiness; the aesthetic spirit cherishes fullness of life, but identifies all too often the good with satisfaction, and, forgetting the stern demands of right, eventuates not infrequently in an unholy happiness. The full Christian fellowship must combine the two: it can and must find a holy happiness. The fact that too often these two aspects of life cannot be reconciled is an indication of an evil dichotomy between the two which must be healed. Liberal evangelicalism may provide the needed synthesis of these two fundamental tendencies.

A liberal evangelicalism is, it is maintained, possible. The permanent values of liberalism such as tolerance, patience, humility, belief in freedom, can be organically combined with the positive values of evangelical positiveness, the firmness of faith's convictions, and an absolute trust in God. How is this possible? Religiously we can unreservedly accept Jesus as God and Savior if with that is meant that Jesus truly revealed the nature and will of God to create by the Christian Cross a full and free fellowship based on a self-transcending, uncalculating, God-given love. The absoluteness of the Christian revelation is in its picture of God as being love, not in a cosmic fashion, turned away from evil as in Neo-Platonism, but in the Christian sense, where the holy God, because He is love, willingly suffers to save the sinner and create with him and through Himself a new order of fellowship. If Jesus is, in this sense, God and Savior, because his self-sacrificing life and death and his teachings to the same effect are saving the world so that there is truly no other name given whereby man must be saved, we liberals cannot but wholeheartedly accept this formula. This faith is more than an attitude; it is a definite principle for interpretation, applicable in every field of theological and social interpretation, whether metaphysically, ethically, or socially. With this view of the Christian Revelation, earnest seekers of the liberal tradition can completely comply; while it ought equally to satisfy the most conservative, since it preserves deeply every fundamental of Christian faith, namely that God was in Christ reconciling Himself unto the world.

If this view of the Revelation and the dependence on man for its application in concrete situations is accepted, then absolute emotional commitment to Christ is possible, while fanaticism is inevitably avoided. By reason alone on ordinary experience, man cannot find the Christian God. The history of philosophy ought to prove that contention. The Revelation is a historical "given," ultimately a mystery; and yet reason must be used to interpret that givenness in every

situation. Since, moreover, we as men know ourselves to be fallible, and since our reason, if Christian, must be directed through love, there is not
only ample room but a complete necessity for
that liberality, tolerance, humility, and freedom
which is not based on the self-sufficiency of man.
It is just for this reason that some liberals consider
Schleiermacher their greatest representative, for
he theologically, even if not methodologically,
made God central and made dependence on Him
the fundamental religious attitude. Christian love
always depends upon its divine source and from
it seeks wisdom through worship and through
the highest possible freedom and fullness in
Christian fellowship.

Jesus seems concretely to have combined the
two attitudes. At times his message is apocalyptic,
demanding absolute commitment even unto
death. "Let the dead bury their dead." His
prophetism is startling and seemingly impossible
in its rigor. Yet Jesus came also to bring completeness of life. He evidently enjoyed the wisdom literature in the Greek spirit and quoted it
approvingly. He saw with joy the children, the

birds, and the flowers. He was accused of loose living, of failing to be strict; and yet he went to the Cross. He saw the good in the Samaritan and in the father receiving his prodigal son; and yet he could rebuke in scathing terms the sins of self-satisfaction and of the hardened heart. There is a liberalism in Jesus which is not modernized interpretation, in his life, in his method, in his teachings; and yet he is our symbol of the absolute, of the unmitigated crisis of life.

We who are his followers must, then, be liberal evangelicals. We must be religiously committed absolutely and unquestioningly to the Christian love of God as the supreme revelation of reality and as the highest ideal for fellowship. Yet we must not become self-satisfied, narrow, or fanatical with regard to this truth, but must ever recognize that our human reason cannot initiate this revelation, cannot fully comprehend it, cannot completely interpret it, nor yet with full wisdom apply it. There is much light yet to be shed from it and there are ever new historical needs to be met. To-day it is easy to join the crowd in discarding with superior airs the liberal truths won by the cross of many saintly lives; it is harder, however, to do without the best in liberalism as an ideal. Liberalism when dissociated from man's false pride, that very liberalism which history has now condemned, means humility and tolerance; it means that all literalisms and institutionalisms are human in nature, that Christian fellowship must ever cherish freedom, that the Christian Church must have ample capacity for a prophetic individualism that will not be fanatical but fruitful for fellowship, that only one thing is absolutely certain and never to be questioned, much less denied, namely that God has revealed Himself in Jesus as redemptive love, that the world is lost without this God-centered love, and that we as a Christian Church must make it more fully ours, so that a new evangelism will burst forth, positive, earnest, victorious, until the Cross of Christ receive its crown, the eternal freedom and fullness in fellowship, the glorified Church of God.

V

The Kingdom of God and the Christian Church

ONE of the basic problems confronting our Christian fellowship is a divided Christendom. The ecumenical movement offers a solution. If church union, however, is to be a matter of conviction and not merely a question of expediency, the organic unity of the Christian Church must depend upon its relation to the more than historical reality of the Kingdom of God. Although the prevalent idea that people, being of different psychological types, cannot by their very nature permanently worship together, and the idea that social and historical differences make an effective union impossible, are believed in certain circles to be sober realism, these assertions, besides being unhistorical, amount to the denial of the divine nature of the Christian

[132]

Church. While we hold such low ideas of the Church, the deeper union can never be consummated, nor indeed, before we have the vision, not only emotionally but also intellectually, of the Christian Church as the essential embodiment of the Christian faith.

Since, moreover, no progress can be made by the giving up of any doctrine felt to be specifically entrusted to us by God Himself, the body of Christ can become one in fact as well as in spirit only through a patient growth, not only in love, but also in understanding. The deepest difficulty with our doctrines of the Christian Church is an undue simplification of its nature. In every theological position concerning the Church there is usually a fallacious abstraction, especially since there are at least three inevitable aspects of any adequate doctrine of the Church. To have an understanding of the Church that at all approximates the reality for which it stands, it may be helpful to think of it in terms of the Eastern formula for the procession of the Holy Ghost. The Kingdom of God corresponds to God the Father. Even as He, beyond clear human understanding, is the transcendent source of all ideal embodiment, so the Kingdom of God is the foundational reality of the Christian Church Catholic. This, in turn, may be compared to the Son. Even as the Son is the embodiment of the Father, so the Christian Church Catholic is the extension of the Incarnation, of the invisible rule of grace through the succession of saints, of the mystical body of Christ. The Christian Church Corporate, again, corresponds to the Holy Spirit. Even as it, though itself of God, perfect and absolute, works through the media of sinful men and of sinful institutions, so the divided churches represent not only the Kingdom of God, the source of their divine dignity, but also the fallible, sinful conditions of men. Even as the Holy Spirit is Christ with us to the end of the World, the sinless eternal Deity present in our sinful humanity, so the Christian Church Corporate even in its state of humiliation is of infinite importance because it is, in spite of the imperfections on its human side, the embodiment of the Church Catholic, the eternal, transcendent Kingdom of God present in the historic flux of human fallibility.

The source of our difficulty in thinking about the Christian Church is our failure to incorporate correctly and proportionately all these necessary aspects. We need both high-church and low-church emphasis, for the high churchman is inevitably uncompromisingly right, in his view of the Christian Church as an end, as a suprahistorical reality directly expressing the will of God. He is also right in his insistence that the Church must be the direct and visible continuation of the Consciousness of Christ. The low churchman, on the other hand, is no less right in his contention that the visible church or churches be viewed as fallible, historic institutions, as means to the Kingdom of God. To confound the visible churches with the Kingdom of God, and especially to equate them, would be spiritually disastrous. To lose the emphasis of either the absolute or the relative, the eternal or the historical, would be to lose the meaning of the Incarnation and to forfeit the mystery of the Christian Gospel of God's perfection being in a sinful world. The separate investigation of these aspects of the Church will reveal both their necessity and the confusion of thought regarding them which has obstructed the historic embodiment of that spiritual unity which in ecumenical gatherings has been much further experienced than expressed.

The Kingdom of God, like God the Father, is transcendent in nature. When religion loses its dimension of transcendence, it loses its depth. Christianity is essentially a mystery, the mystery of the Cross. This mystery, however, disappears when God is Himself reduced to the terms of human thinking. The early Christians knew what the mystery of the Gospel meant. Christianity has always been in danger, however, of losing this stress. When man acquires that intellectual pride which pretends to know the richness and the fullness of the ways of God, religion becomes thin and ineffective. Only when man becomes humble enough to accept God's redemptive acts in history as a drama too superhuman in nature for him to understand more than through a glass darkly is the deepest worship possible. In our human self-sufficiency we have reduced the ways of God to our own understanding, limited Him by our view of the good;

we have taken Him into account before the judgment seat of our little understanding based on our little knowledge of our infinitely short history in our infinitely small world. Whenever the sense of the hidden God is lost through the light of the revealed God, the intensity of our religious emotions tends to fade away and we live mostly on inherited spiritual capital. Wholesome is the stress on the otherness of God without which religion cannot overpower and control the human heart.

The Kingdom of God, similarly, transcends history, but imparts to history its meaning in the light of God's eternal purpose, namely to create and redeem a fellowship where His will is freely and faithfully carried out in heaven and on earth, where the Spirit of Christ rules supreme in the hearts of men. The meaning of this is but partly understood and experienced on earth. The Kingdom of God for Jesus was to be brought by God in His own time and in His own way; and even though he felt himself to be a part of it, its inmost secrets were not even for him. The early Christians had a vivid sense of the difference between the Kingdom of God and their present situation. The Kingdom to which they belonged was yet to be fulfilled by the inscrutable Will of God. To lose this stress on the Kingdom is tantamount to losing the stress on the transcendence of God. For this reason, the apparent Roman Catholic identification of the Kingdom and the visible Church forfeits an indispensable aspect of the Christian Church. To equate the Kingdom with the world, of course, and thus with the progressive amelioration of human society, or completely to confound the ways of God with the ways of man, is much less adequate than the Catholic position, for this is to lose even more the sense of the eternal beyond the temporal. The Catholic stress on the Church as founded in the Kingdom of God, as an end beyond all human ends, is necessary, but its view of the mystery of the Kingdom of God and the way God works in history is defective. Either to deny that the Church finds its deepest reality in the Kingdom of God transcending human history, or to affirm that the Kingdom of God can be fully understood in terms of a visible human institution, or in terms of social ideals, is to lose an essential element in the doctrines of the Church. The stress on this transcendent element, however, must not blind us to the fact that there are also two historic aspects of the Church which, receiving their meaning from the Kingdom of God, are, nevertheless, not to be identified with it.

The first of these two aspects is the Christian Church Catholic, which we have compared to the Son. The mystery of the Son has always been a stumbling-block to the Church. There has been through the history of Christian thought a stream of attempts to deny his full embodiment. Many religious souls, devout followers of the Master, have found it difficult to accept the most basic thought of the Christian religion, namely that the eternal itself becomes historical, that the perfect enters the imperfect, that the spiritual becomes one without confusion with the natural, that the sinless suffers with and for sin. If Jesus was truly man, in the way that any one of us is, they say, he was not truly God. To save the fact that God was in him they resort to what amounts to a denial of his full embodiment. There has also been a contrary stream denying that the fullness of the Father was in the Son. This flow of thought has emphasized that Jesus exemplified the divine rather than that God became flesh. The study of these two opposing streams reveals that men in some way find it easy to remove Jesus either from God or from man. The simple thought that Jesus reveals what God is as far as He has been revealed within human history is not sufficient for those who wish to live by their own thoughts rather than by the Revelation of God in Christ Jesus.

In the same way as the Son is the Incarnation of the Father, so the Christian Church Catholic is the ideal embodiment in human history of the Kingdom of God. The Christian Church is not an accident in human affairs; it is not primarily a matter of historical development; but it is the real continuation of the spirit of Christ, a segment of the deepest reality of eternity partially present but embodied in all its reality in the Christian Church Catholic. It is the invisible church present through the visible church, but

not to be identified with it; for it is the fellowship of all Christians in the state of grace, the
redeemed society through the act of God, and
fully known to Him alone. As the Son receives
his meaning through the transcendent Father, so
the Christian Church Catholic receives its meaning through the Kingdom of God beyond human
history. In this sense the Church is an end, the
eternal end within time. The Church is fellowship among God and men in the spirit of Christ.
This is the meaning of history; this is our fullest
understanding of eternity. Beyond this we can
know nothing. Yet one of our tragedies is always
to live in the future. We become so interested in
the means of community, God-given though
they are, that we have little time for or concern
with the fellowship itself, either with God or
with men. Wherever there is fellowship with
God in the spirit of Christ and through God with
men, there is present the Christian Church Catholic. This fellowship is most usual through worship. To reduce worship to a means, however, is
to destroy the end of all things, the finality of
that fellowship which is the Kingdom of God.

When men partake of the Eucharist or bow in prayer before God, there takes place something worth while for its own sake, an intrinsically good experience. Life's deepest experience, its highest end, is to feel the presence of God and the love of man in penitence, forgiveness, and thanksgiving. To deny this is to invite skepticism, to deny the objective reality of the Kingdom of God through the Church. In this we agree with Hocking when he writes: "Unless there is an immediately felt meaning, there is no meaning at all: no future meaning could compensate for a complete absence of meaning in the present moment; and whatever meaning life may come to possess hereafter must be simply the ampler interpretation of the meaning which it now has."[1] In order to guard the truth that the Church is an end, it is important to understand that just as the Son proceeds from God the Father in a historic ideal fullness, which must never be confused with the Father, so the Christian Church Catholic proceeds from the Kingdom of God in an ideal fullness which must,

[1] Hocking: *Thoughts on Death and Life*, p. 226.

[142]

nevertheless, never be confused with the eternal fullness of the transcendent Kingdom. From the Christian Church Catholic then proceeds the Christian Church Corporate.

The real confusion arises when the relation between the Church Catholic and the Church Corporate is not clear. The Church Catholic is God's Kingdom on earth, the universal dominion of which is heaven, the unchangeable reality of which it is death to deny. The Church Corporate, on the other hand, is a means, the fallible expression of the Church within the relativities of history's dynamic advance. Just as the Holy Spirit of God is itself perfect and yet operative in a sinful world, so the Church, insofar as it represents God's Spirit, is infallible, but insofar as it represents the efforts of men, is touched with human imperfection. God's Holy Spirit is truly present in a history which knows no embodied perfection; the Christian Church Corporate is similarly both of God and imperfect. History is not perfect because God has given men freedom, and works by His grace through that freedom. History represents the joint creation of God and

His creative creatures. Since God never imposes His will arbitrarily or artificially on history, the Christian Church Corporate is touched with all the imperfections by which human institutions reflect the imperfection of the human spirit. Man's mistake is that by considering the embodied forms perfect he confounds the work of God with the work of man. The only rule for the Christian Church Corporate is that it express as fully as possible the Spirit of Christ, which is love's loyalty to God and to the principles of His Kingdom. The form must never deny the unity of the Spirit; the Church Corporate must never deny the Church Catholic; for by so doing it also denies the Kingdom which is its only claim to its divine origin and nature. Oneness in Christ must involve both active cooperation and wide difference of expression. The Church Catholic is a concrete universal capable of complete inner unity through varied outward difference. Church union then becomes not a matter of external uniformity, but a universal cooperation in the quest for the fuller understanding and the spreading of the Gospel, and the common struggle against evil through whatever forms best comply with our concrete historic situation.

The coming of an effective church union thus has as its prerequisite the deeper understanding of the nature of the Christian Church in all its aspects, that institution which even though its form has been fashioned by the ways of history is itself above history; for although there will be neither State nor family in heaven, the Church, being by its very nature a part of God's eternal Kingdom, will never be abrogated or superseded, but only expanded and fulfilled.

VI

Symbolism and Sacramental Theory

HISTORICALLY, the sacraments are at the heart of Christian worship. Because of a seemingly unacceptable theology which developed around them, however, a large part of the Christian Church, even though it usually practices some form of sacramental worship, has become decidedly non-sacramental in attitude and theory. To-day, however, a substantial number of leaders within this non-sacramental tradition are anxious for an examination of the whole subject: some because they dread the present turn to liturgy without a deeper understanding that worship must be grounded in theology; some because they see sacramental theory as one of the main obstacles in the way of an effective church union; some because they believe that even though the specific historic forms of sacramental theory may be unacceptable, they must in view of the intensity of feeling connected with them stand for some vital truth.

Of these the first group contains many who hope that a thorough study of the subject will reveal that sacramental worship is inconsistent with direct Protestant spirituality, while others of their number are merely bewildered and basically open-minded on the subject. The real drive to rethink the problem, however, comes from the second and third groups. The second group has a real purpose behind its determination to investigate sacramental theory. It sees in the ecumenical movement the promise of the reunion of the Christian Church. With high hopes it sees signs of our passing from what Congar called *Divided Christendom* to what Mersch, after Augustine, so meaningfully entitled *The Whole Christ*. More and more thinkers have come to feel that there will never be a unity of faith before every part of the Christian Church ceases to think in terms of historic difference and possible compromise and sees instead the problems in the light of the essentials of faith which, once they are adequately understood, must by their very nature necessarily unite us all. Most of our difficulties are due to our inability to see the questions of faith in the balance of truth, to our unwholesome exaggeration of some aspect of it, and to our individualistic unwillingness to have our insights supplemented and corrected by other thinkers. We have gone each his own way, often under the influence of some secular thinker, and have neglected vitally to interpret our doctrines, particularly those of history and nature, in the light of the metaphysical presuppositions of the Christian faith itself. Church union is hindered because many of us in the non-sacramental tradition have accepted secular philosophies wherein history and nature have been interpreted with practically no sense that God Himself constitutes the final principle of explanation. A false dichotomy between spirit and nature has become part and parcel of our thinking. Non-sacramentalism has failed to appreciate the effects of the physical on the spiritual. To assure direct access to God it has to a great extent, especially in theory, denied the indirect means by which God enters and nourishes the soul. To vindicate its belief in the priesthood of all believers it has dismissed as ecclesiastical and institutional the necessary historic channeling of God's grace. To assure God's immediate presence it has dangerously underestimated the usual necessity for historic mediation. To make the soul primary in its theological interpretation it has detrimentally neglected the body. In this chapter, therefore, we shall deal with two of the theological problems that particularly stand in the way of church union as far as sacramental theory is concerned: How can saving grace be transmitted through history, and how can God be really present by means of material media?

Both this second group that desires an investigation of sacramental theory in order to make church union possible and the third group, which feels that the power which sacramental worship has had throughout the history of the Christian Church must be due to some vital truth, are greatly helped both by the new way of looking at theological problems provided by the philosophy of organism and by a new interpretation of history. Traditional theology has been expressed to a large extent in terms of a substance philosophy which failed to do justice to Christian faith. Because of this philosophy, doctrines like transubstantiation, consubstantiation, virtualism, and receptionism became formulated. This way of looking at the problem has become almost irrelevant to those who think in terms of the philosophy of organism. The Christian stress on personality as ultimate can be more adequately understood and expressed in terms of a reality which is through and through a living process than in terms of a philosophy where nature is so self-sufficient that a miracle must happen in order for God to be present in it. We are also coming to think of history as a living process. The nineteenth century, because it gave us a critical method for historic research, is often named the historical century; but the important part about history is not its pastness but its activity as a conditioning element in the present. George Herbert Meade rightly maintains that the present is the locus of reality. Tillich stresses the future reference in the historical consciousness. Dewey points out that each present is conditioned by its relevant past while at the same time each present to a great degree also selects its relevant past. Whitehead understands the meaning of history as the effect of the settled hand of the past in the present, but makes ample allowance for the choice by each present moment of decision of its particularly relevant past. This is perhaps indication enough as to how history is being understood more and more in organic, functional terms. What has been done in the past is now understood by the very nature of history to be an active element in the formation of the present, and as we shall see later, not only by means of man's conscious thought but through the whole process of historical inheritance. It is factors like these which can move Quick to write that "the intellectual earthquakes of the last century have shifted all the old landmarks."[1] It is interpretations like these which make those who desire church union and those who in any case wish to rethink the problems involved in sacramental theory hopeful that a new way of looking at the

[1] Quick, *The Christian Sacraments*, p. 207.

old, seemingly unanswerable questions may be able both to conserve and to make generally acceptable the deepest truth underlying the historic doctrines.

It is becoming increasingly apparent that the depreciation of history by much of Protestant theology has been unrealistic. To be sure, this theology has usually appealed to a historic Person and a historic event. Its doctrine of redemption, nevertheless, has been mostly atomistic, with God forgiving each sinner directly because of the historic work of Jesus Christ. Even though certain satisfaction theories of the Atonement along with some nominalistic interpretations of the ways of God in history could account for the relation between historic Calvary and present personal salvation; nevertheless, an organic interpretation of historic continuity constitutes a more adequate explanation. Those who make the unique the essence of history are unrealistic because they make it impossible even to investigate history. Without some continuity of common elements, without some conformation of past to present forms, history would be uninterpretable. Some recurrence is necessary for recognizability, and recognizability is necessary for knowledge. Even though one important function of history is differentiation, it is quite misleading to say with Moses that "the unique and non-repeatable is the essence of history."[2] The particular facts of history would be inaccessible to the historian if there were no universal, enduring elements which provided a basis for understanding and comparison. Apart from an understanding of in what sense history is a continuum, there can be no vital comprehension of an adequate sacramental theory.

Since Christianity is intrinsically a kind of fellowship between God and man which is itself the end of all its desires and endeavors, the function of the sacrament, its means of grace, can only be to perpetuate, expand, unify, and deepen the Christian fellowship. Historically, the Christian Church is a new community. Whatever be our point of view as to whether Jesus did or did not formally found the Christian Church and in-

[2] Moses, "The Problem of Truth in Religion," in *The Authority of the Faith*, p. 78.

stitute the sacraments, it seems indisputable that through him a new kind of fellowship came into being. From the earliest times there were certain signs connected with the incorporation into this community and the continuation in it. This fellowship, moreover, was believed to be maintained by means of supernatural grace. Arthur Darby Nock correctly observes this truth: "There are moreover fundamental differences in pagan and Christian sacraments. Pagan sacraments turn on the liberating or creating of an immortal element in the individual with a view to the hereafter but with no effective change of the moral self for the purposes of living. Christian sacraments, in their earliest phase, turned entirely on corporate participation in the new order, for which all were alike unfitted by nature."[3] Unless it be granted at the outset that God did something in Christ which the Church is peculiarly instituted to transmit, it is useless to discuss the sacraments in the historic sense. We may differ as to what God did. The view of the

[3] Nock, "Mysteries," in *The Encyclopedia of the Social Sciences*, Vol. XI, p. 174.

writer is that He revealed and made possible a new kind of fellowship. The real question, however, for those of us who use sacramental symbolism, though we speak of ordinances, is in what sense we can accept an affirmation like Congar's: "This incorporation in Christ is begun and effected—and this is all important . . . by contact with Christ in the sacramental order."[4] This presentation takes the point of view that the sacraments are means of grace in virtue of that symbolic principle of historic existence through which the significant rites of any fellowship are actually means of its continuity and of the promotion of its purposes. In a most effectual sense God's grace is conveyed by means of sacramental symbolism. This affirmation naturally calls for specific explanation.

Our first question is how the Christian Church can perpetuate, expand, and deepen its peculiar kind of fellowship by means of the sacraments. It must, in the first place, be kept in mind that all derivation from the past is formed and colored. History knows of no *materia prima*. All

---

[4] Congar, *Divided Christendom*, p. 62.

historical heritage has some degree of structure. Some of the forms of history are organic unities, particularly those characterizing living societies. Such societies possess peculiar possibilities for experience which can never be obtained anywhere else. They thus provide what Spens called "a complex of persisting opportunities of experience."[5] The Christian Church is so integrally related to a definite form of fellowship, to what Whitehead would call "a complex eternal object," that apart from participation in its historic concretion its full reality cannot be experienced. By the principle of relevancy every present is conditioned by its past and partially conforms to it. It is easily observable, moreover, that most derivation from the past is on the physical plane below the level of conscious choice or distinct awareness. Poor would be our lives if we were to depend entirely on our taking thought. The physical processes of life go on without constant conscious volition. On any level our deliberate appropriation from the past would be thin and

[5] Spens, "The Eucharist" in *Essays Catholic and Critical*, p. 441, note.

trivial. Throughout all of life operates an *ex opere operato* principle. The past is more than given to us; it hurls itself at us. This is what Whitehead means when he stresses that the fundamental mode of derivation from the past is that of "causal efficacy." Whenever the Christian fellowship is transmitted through time, the whole fellowship on a deep conditioning level beyond explicit recognition is reproduced in its new members; it is, so to speak, recapitulated in terms of that specific past which molds incoming individuals in a historic corporate society of constantly overlapping selves. Those within the fellowship of the Church have thus the past of an organic structure forming their immediate present. In other words, what Christ did and what the Church has been become in the very nature of things a constitutive part of their very lives. In this sense the very life of the Church is truly poured into the individual believer. Something older and larger than himself lives, to a great extent, his very life. "This do in memory of me" is more than a pious exhortation to conscious recall; it is the very lifeblood of faith. We are what we are organically as a Christian fellowship because of what God did through Christ and what God has continued to do through the Church. What has been done comes to life in us on a level much deeper than our conscious creation. The life of the Church is a vehicle of continuing grace far stronger than the clear faith or active goodness of any or all of its members. On that deep level of causal efficacy God works in the historic fellowship of the Church beyond the power of our complete understanding or effective resolve.

Observe the realistic sense in which physical acts effect spiritual consequences. How did our own lives come to be apart from physical causes? What can be less rational and more naturalistic than physical conception? And yet we dare to believe that along with it somehow came to be a human soul with spiritual reality and destiny. Whether the soul is transduced or created makes no difference in this instance, for in any case a distinctly spiritual reality became joined to a physical process. Similarly, how did we grow if not in conjunction with a body historically inseparable from the self? This, moreover, grew by means of physical food, water, and air, by continually appropriating and exchanging with a physical environment. If spiritual life here depends upon the eating of physical food, if the spirit in this life is dependent upon the body, why cannot bread and wine offered by the Church in Christ's name constitute spiritual food effective of spiritual grace? We must at least recognize that by means of physical acts the very fellowship of life is effected and maintained, that God uses the natural in order gradually to produce the spiritual. In all fairness, in any case, we must admit that it is not those who retreat in horror from natural causation in the spiritual life who are realistic, but those who see how the physical does affect the spiritual in the life that we do know. When we correctly grasp the relation of the physical to the psychical, of the natural to the spiritual, we may find with A. A. Bowman that we live in a *Sacramental Universe*.

According to the view of history that we have advanced, historical transmission operates to a great extent on the physical level in an *ex opere operato* manner. On this level, basic continuity is

[159]

consistent with historic differentiation. All of the past is hurled into the present, but our relevant past depends upon the historic societies of which we are members. It must not be gathered from our discussion so far, however, that transmission is altogether on this level. On the very contrary, significant transmission is effected by means of symbolism, or by means of abstraction from the fullness of the past. Most of the past enters as a vague background into present consciousness; something of the past is translated, to be sure, into clear ideas, but such part of it as is meaningfully apprehended is done so by means of symbols which reproduce and generally suggest that great reality which cannot be adequately grasped in terms of distinct ideas. This level Whitehead calls "presentational immediacy" and insists that in order to preserve the insights and the power of the past it is necessary to find the correct symbols and apply them to the needs of the present. It seems well to restate this important principle which is crucial to our thesis: All of existence enters into the mode of causal efficacy, that is, all existence becomes the general background of

every present, but every present experient selects or "abstracts" from this totality certain parts
of it by its own activity of choice in the mode
of "presentational immediacy." This immediate
content of his awareness would, however, be
thin and powerless apart from the experient's relating himself meaningfully by means of "symbolic reference" to that dim background of experience which contains the richness of life.
All significant historical transmission is, consequently, by means of effective symbolism. The
whole of the Church's past hurls itself into our
present but can be significantly appropriated
only by means of symbolic reference. We must
recognize that it is the habit of most people to
live by what Hegel called "materialized thinking."[6] In this respect Archbishop Temple is right
when he affirms that "in the physical universe
symbolism is the principle of existence."[7] This
explains the power of sacramental worship, for
where can one find such effective symbols as the
Christian sacraments? The sacraments, by sym-

[6] *Hegel's Phenomenology of Mind* (J. B. Baillie, translator),
p. 117.
[7] Temple, *Christ the Truth*, p. 300.

[161]

bolizing the historic realities by which the Church lives, are also instrumental in realizing them. The test of a Christian sacrament, therefore, is its power to make vital, meaningful, and effective the historic faith by which the Church lives. The Roman Catholics are right when they define the sacraments as effective symbols of God's grace through Christ. They are inadequate in their understanding of sacramental efficacy. The miracle of the sacraments is the miracle of all high grades of experience. The liberals are right when they define the sacraments as "aids to the imagination"; but they are wrong when they deny that God works through them in a peculiarly effective manner to convey His grace. The sacraments make it particularly possible to experience the forgiveness of God and by means of it to enter more vitally into Christian fellowship. When we understand the principle of symbolic reference we also can understand how by means of the sacraments the great gift of God through Christ and the Church is particularly perpetuated in the reality of the Christian fellowship.

The view of history that we have advanced stresses both the historical Event and the continuity of the work of grace. It emphasizes that the Church as a special vehicle of the Spirit transmits grace in a special manner that cannot be found outside it. This claim, moreover, has been founded not on any arbitrary assertion of authority, but on the very nature of historic transmission pertaining to living societies. Outside active fellowship in the Christian Church there can never be an adequate experience of that new kind of community for which man is destined and outside which he can never find his truest self. Naturally, our view rejects as superficial the notion that the continuity of the Church is in terms of external, arbitrary succession, and stresses instead the living continuity of a kind of fellowship centered in God and made possible through Jesus Christ.

It is well to be clear on this point. Our stress on the physical as the medium of transmission easily might be misunderstood. If the physical is itself the primary mode of derivation from the past, it ought to follow that the visible church or at least the institutional embodiment of the church must also be primary. If this were so, we should have to arrive at a doctrine where the organized Christian community, the visible institution as such, by means of its possession of the specific past of the distinctively Christian Church would alone provide the possibility for Christian fellowship. Naturally, the embodied form ought to possess the unity of its ideal; the embodied form of Christianity ought to possess organizational unity. Nevertheless, in the organic philosophy which we are using as a medium of interpretation, the ideal is always primary, the mind is directive of the body. It must not be gathered, therefore, from our stress on the physical nature of historic transmission that the physical is independent of the ideal. Not only the body of the Church but also its mind, not only its material or organizational content but also its spiritual forms and feelings are confirmed in the present. Formed physical confirmation is in fact because of and by means of the spiritual which is always primary. Even though transmission is via the physical, what is significant is the ideal which has taken

[164]

form in the physical. God's full ideal for fellowship He alone knows, but our highest knowledge of it came through the life of Jesus Christ. It is this ideal and the saving power which can be conveyed through it as it remains embodied in the living community of the Christian Church which matters. The degree of physical embodiment can be measured by the spiritual, but not *vice versa*. When we thus speak of derivation from the past in the mode of causal efficacy we always mean a formed past, a history with structure in it, a material molded by the spirit. Efficient causation, insofar as it enters history, contains the embodiment of final causation in the past. Even though the ideal is ever future in its fullness it has to some extent impressed itself on the past. The relevance of a dynamic ideal to any given present is, in fact, proportionate to its embodiment in the past. What God did in Christ thus conditions every present of the Church, not entirely by means of specific institutional embodiment, but by means of that ideal which once in known history is accessible to men. The Christ of faith is thus needed as well as the Christ of history. This explains how even though the Church exists only as an imperfect fellowship as far as its actual expression in the world is concerned, even to the point where one may question exactly where it is; nevertheless it is in essence, both historically and in the continuity of the communion of saints, that is, of those who through all ages have made this fellowship central in their allegiance and affection, a living reality. The invisible church needs the visible church; every ideal needs an institution, or some embodied form, to perpetuate it. The physical continuity, however, receives its significance through its carrying of the spiritual reality which is its own standard.

From our discussion it therefore follows that wherever men have fellowship in the spirit and faith of Christ there is a Christian Church. In proportion to its making Christ and his kind of fellowship central, subordinating all differences of historic form to him and to his prayer that all be one, a church takes on more fully the character of the Church. Surely, fellowship based on the love of God as revealed in Christ Jesus is a wide enough category to include all differences not directly inconsistent with that spirit. When the Spirit of Christ dominates his Body the problem of effective administration can be mastered in time. "Drink ye all of it" surely applies to all who honestly desire to profess and practice the Christian fellowship.

If the part of the individual seems to have been underemphasized in this account of history, our answer must be that no final efficacy is achieved through the sacraments apart from the necessary mode of presentational immediacy where the significance of the Christian fellowship becomes operative in the individual. Pourrat feels that the Protestant doctrine emphasizes the ethical far too much. "It is because a sacrament has no other purpose than that of exciting faith, that, according to the Protestants, sacramental theories are exhortatory, not consecratory. The sacred ceremony consists chiefly in an exhortation: a sacrament is a kind of acted sermon which keeps up the faith of the subject."[8] The point of view of the present writer, however, is that the consecratory and the exhortatory cannot be separated. It

[8] Pourrat, *Theology of the Sacraments,* p. 179.

is God who gives His grace through the Church to the individual, but unless it eventuates in his entering into a deeper fellowship, the sacrament is of no avail. The ethical is an inseparable part of genuine sacramental worship. If the spirit is active it must bear fruit. Archbishop Temple writes: "The proof that we have received the Presence is the increase of love in our daily lives. . . . If a man goes out from his Communion to love and serve men better he has received the Real Presence. If he feels every thrill and tremor of devotion, but goes out as selfish as before, he has not received it. It was offered, but he did not receive it."[9] Naturally, we are vitally concerned with the results in each individual, but since the sacraments refer primarily to the fellowship, the dominant stress in sacramental theory must be on the corporate continuity by which God promotes His historic purposes.

To the question as to how Christ can be specially present in the sacraments, several answers may be given. We have already suggested how the physical mode of existence carries and affects

[9] Temple, *op. cit.*, pp. 228 and 299.

the spiritual. When, however, it is stated that since Christ is already present everywhere, a special presence is unnecessary, we must understand that such a position involves indiscriminate pantheism. With a true feeling for Christian verities Spens writes: "The idea of a special presence of God would seem to be in itself one with which religion cannot dispense."[10] Even if we accept panentheism in the sense that God is everywhere present in some manner, we believe, nevertheless, that He is also specially present in different places under different conditions. If we were to accept a form of mathematical mysticism, we could say that the sacraments provide certain patterns which transmit a certain consciousness of God otherwise not attainable. A competent modern thinker like Whitehead teaches that forms condition consciousness. There are, however, other possible explanations. If our bodies, as Hocking holds, are the means by which we insert ourselves into nature, then the sacraments may be one way in which God especially visits the Church in visible form. Or if nature is thought of

[10] Spens, *op. cit.,* p. 439.

as God's consciousness organized in particular manners for particular purposes, as a medium of embodied ideas through which God converses with us in some such way as that suggested by Berkeley, then it may be that God in His wisdom has chosen the sacraments through which particularly to present Himself according to His promises to those who obey His commands and accept the authority of that fellowship which He has Himself instituted for man's salvation. Or if "body" is interpreted more realistically as our environment organized in a most relevant manner, to use another of Whitehead's ideas, "this is my body" can be explained as Christ's special environment for the particular purpose of man's salvation through the Church. There are thus many ways of explaining the category of nature presupposed in sacramental theory. The writer, however, makes the Christian fellowship itself so central that Christ is taken to be particularly present through the sacraments just because by means of their symbolic power the reality of the Christian fellowship is experienced at its deepest and fullest level. God's grace comes to us as the experience of this fellowship through the forgiveness of sin. God's redemptive activity in the past, in the present, and for the future ("this do till he come") finds us in the very depths of our lives when we worship sacramentally. Since the purpose of Creation is the establishing of the order of fellowship between God and man, and men and men, God is naturally present in it in a sense that He cannot be outside it. No individual worshipping by himself, and no group that has not the sense of the full Christian fellowship can experience God in the way in which He is experienced in the sacraments.

The aim of this study in sacramental theory has been the constructive investigation of the doctrines of history and nature in their relation to the historic faith. Because God works in a special way through the Christian Church, we do not deny but confidently affirm that He works also in other ways. The source and standard of sacramental theory is the Christian fellowship. Whatever group makes that primary both in profession and practice, even though, like the Society of Friends, it refuse to use the sacramental symbolism of the historic Church, nevertheless is to be tested by its spiritual fruits, by its kind of fellowship. We cannot conceive of the sacraments as being a principle of division and of exclusion in a truly Christian community. We do think that when fellowship becomes primary and the means are seen in their proper place, when all ideas of idolatry and magic are resolutely banished from sacramental theory and worship, the whole Church will be helped, not hindered, by sacramental symbolism. Non-sacramental groups have protested against sacramentalism to the detriment of their own ordinances. Much will be done to further sacramental worship in our churches when history is understood as the organic channel of special grace through a distinct order of fellowship rather than as the arbitrary container of grace limited to a Church resting its claim to exclusive continuity on external authority. We rejoice, therefore, when our Roman Catholic friends call us "separated brethren," affirming that we are not heretics, that we belong not only to the soul of the Church but also to its body, even though in a different manner from

[172]

them.[11] We ought all to admit that no group can claim to have the full experience of Christ's whole body until the perfect freedom and faithfulness in Christ's fellowship is achieved, and that the visible Church is broken because of our common failure to incarnate constructively and forgivingly the Spirit of Christ. When seen in the full light of the Kingdom of God we cannot claim, any of us, to be members of the full reality, but, pleading God's help and mercy, we feel that in this historic order we are all members both *in re* and *in voto*.[12]

This chapter has suggested that we non-sacramentarians have been unrealistic and inadequate in our view of history and nature. The saving power which came into the world through Jesus Christ has been effectively passed on through his Church on a very fundamental level by sacramental symbolism. We are thankful to our Catholic brethren for their preserving this truth while

[11] Congar, *op. cit.*, Chapter 7, "The Status of Our Separated Brethren."

[12] This, of course, refers to the Roman Catholic formula describing the status of those baptized believers who are not members of the Roman Catholic Church: *membra non in re sed in voto*.

it was especially obnoxious to the spirit of the age. We hope and pray for that final unity which we know must come when God is placed above every institution, though not so as to minimize its authority and importance; when the spirit is placed above the letter, though not so as to deny its value and necessity; when freedom in fellowship is placed above external authority and historic order, though not so as to refuse recognition of their proper usefulness and significance. A deeper devotion to Christ will surely convert our differences into merely technical problems of theological interpretation and administrative effectiveness.

VII

Christianity and Karma; the Relation of the Christian Fellowship to a Non-Christian Fellowship

OF UTMOST importance to the Christian Church is its relation to non-Christian faiths. The best way to study the problem is in the light of a concrete religion. In this chapter Christianity and karma are compared to illustrate the relation of the Christian fellowship to non-Christian faiths. Christianity and karma, Hinduism's basic doctrinal tenet, represent two fundamentally different ways of looking at life. Yet they have much to learn from each other.

Any writer who claims that Christianity can learn from another religion ought immediately to clarify his point of view on this issue, which at present is in the very centre of debate. The present writer believes that the fundamental principle of interpretation is not substance nor thought, but personality. For theology, the nature of God as Creator and Redeemer is the basic motif in the light of which all else must be explained. Christianity, as we have seen, is a God-centered, God-given freedom and faithfulness in fellowship based on *agape*, first fully revealed and made effective as light and life in Jesus Christ. If fellowship is fundamental, a constructive comparison of religions is possible both in the realm of ideas and in the realm of living. Only a unity of profession and practice can be fully Christian. But as to the intellectual interpretation of this fellowship based on *agape* we are yet largely in the dark. Practice waits on clearer profession. The theme of this chapter, then, is that Hinduism has certain insights which, hidden beneath conflicting notions, nevertheless witness to the Christian Gospel and can themselves be better understood when seen in the light of Christian truth. Christianity likewise has something to learn from Hinduism, by which to gain a more realistic application of its full faith. The writer's receptivity to certain Hindu insights in no way

[176]

contradicts the conclusion to which a comparison of Christianity with other religions led him:

"The remarkable thing about the Christian idea of love is that it is wide enough to include all forms of fellowship, every kind of communal life. All forms of fellowship can be changed with *agape* as their source and standard. Christianity as the belief in the ultimate victory of a two-dimensional fellowship based on *agape* must, therefore, be effectively related to every kind of fellowship this world has to offer."[1]

Christianity is essentially a religion of grace wherein the natural order of this world seems interrupted by the supernatural intervention of God's forgiveness. The doctrine of karma is essentially the affirmation of the universal sway of the natural order of deed and consequence. Naturally, neither Christianity nor Hinduism is completely consistent with regard to its basic stress, for Christianity has always had a considerable admixture of natural knowledge, whereas Hinduism's doctrine of deliverance at last breaks through the observed laws of phenomenal experi-

[1] *Swedish Contributions to Modern Theology*, pp. 240-241.

ence.[2] Christianity makes the revealed order central and only grudgingly allows empirical considerations, whereas Hinduism makes the natural order doctrinally determinative and then seeks ways to escape from it. Neither the personal nor the natural approach to religion, however, is completely satisfactory. The proper relation between them must be understood and the limitations involved clearly realized.

It is obvious that the struggle between the two views of life is not the old clash between art (*techné*) and chance (*tyché*), but, to a great extent, that between natural uniformity and supernatural Purpose. Our task is to point out that whereas Christianity can make fuller use of the former idea, Hinduism can make room for the latter. Although the idea of karma itself has a fascinating history, and although Christianity and karma can with much profit be studied from many other points of view, for our present purposes the scope of the comparison must neces-

[2] Care should be taken not to identify karma with the scientific concepts of cause and effect. It is rather to be thought of as a moral subconscious operating according to natural laws. A comparison might be made with the old Greek notion of *diké*.

sarily be rigidly limited to the possible relation of natural law and supernatural Purpose in the basic motifs of Christianity, God's redemptive love, and of Hinduism, the uninterrupted, orderly sequence of deed and consequence.

Our first question, then, is whether or not karma as a basic motif has room for what seems, from its point of view, the interference of a transcendent purpose within the natural order. Walter E. Clark stated the problem when he wondered whether the Christian notion of theism did not involve a certain element of caprice.[3] On the other hand, "Karma, 'act,' represents the law of cause and effect, a cosmic regularity, extended from the physical world into the realm of conduct so that it becomes the solution of the moral problem, since the course of one's rebirth depends on the nature of one's acts. This doctrine of karma tends to weaken the theistic element in Indian religion and to strengthen monistic and pantheistic tendencies."[4] "There is always a tendency . . . for Karma to act as a limitation to

[3] Unpublished lectures.
[4] W. E. Clark, "India," in *The Open Court*, Summer, 1933.

God's full sovereignty and grace.''[5] Even though there are in Hinduism theistic sects, the emphasis leads toward the pantheistic sayings symbolic of its deepest thought: "The one without a second"; "thou art that." Our problem is, therefore, how the notion of a God working redeemingly in history can fit into the naturalistic scheme which underlies the doctrine of karma. Our attempt to confront Christianity and karma with each other must, moreover, be in the sphere of the real relation between the natural and the supernatural. In this respect Hinduism presents a basic difficulty which must not be minimized. Hinduism as a religion of redemption merely points to the realm of reality where there are no karmic forces; this, however, is not to solve the problem, but to evade it. It is becoming a strong temptation for many earnest Christian thinkers to do the same. Hinduism is subtly invading a disillusioned and despairing West. Since the two faiths must eventually meet more generally, they ought, as far as possible, to meet on a high intellectual plane where they can learn from each other. Surely the basic

[5] *Ibid.*

[180]

Christian affirmations are both broad enough and deep enough to make effective use of additional light. Karma in this study, therefore, is accepted as having much to suggest with regard to the relation of the spiritual to the natural order. The problem as far as Christianity's contribution to the doctrine of karma is concerned is how to fit into this scheme of deed and consequence the reality of God's effective purposing in history through His redemptive grace.

Fortunately, Hinduism is realistic enough to reject complete determinism. Man is free to change his future by his present conduct. At every moment the cards of life are dealt in accordance with each man's past, but upon his playing of them depends his next hand. "Every sinner has a future even as every saint has a past."[6] This sounds well and good until one realizes that man's experience of his constant failures, which in some doctrinal areas of Christianity has led to the doctrines of original sin and total depravity, has in Hinduism led to a fatalism which makes life itself a thing to be dreaded. Because of

[6] Radhakrishnan: *The Hindu View of Life*, p. 71.

this fatalism, Hinduism must ponder anew that old question which is basic to religion: "Can my soul count on anyone for help?"[7] At this very point, however, Hinduism seems to stand in its own light, for its doctrine of karma leads it needlessly to believe that such help would be contrary to the order of justice, and to cling to an individualism which is both unrealistic and socially inadequate. Hinduism can, nevertheless, have more than a doctrine of redemption through individual deeds and enlightenment. It can become religiously and socially more adequate by adopting a view of God's relation with the world and of social solidarity which seems consistent with its own genius.

Such a solution Shastri's description of the different aspects of karma suggests. "There are three kinds of karma: sancita, prarabdha, and kryamana. The infinite potential, sancita, of an individual becomes prarabdha in its kinetic form, and the working out of these possibilities under proper active circumstances is called kryamana."[8] The pure potentiality becomes actual potential-

---

[7] Moulton: *Early Zoroastrianism*, p. 382, *Yasna* 50.
[8] P. D. Shastri: *The Essentials of Eastern Philosophy*, p. 36.

ity, the formless possibility becomes formed, by
man's present deeds, no matter what may then be
the relation between the irreal, or pure potentiality, the sancita karma, and the impure form, or
prarabdha karma which conditions the present
act. The huge reservoir of man's past is constantly modified by his present. The fact that the
general idea of order, *rita*, has historically become associated with the special idea of *istapurta*,
of merit preceding one to another life, so that
the consequences of one's deeds are usually tied
up in life-bundles and thus not efficacious in the
immediate future, is a secondary historical consideration. The basic idea of karma is that every
deed is followed by its appropriate consequence;
that this is not eternal, but that karma depends on
ever new deeds. The relation between deed and
consequence, moreover, is not on a quantitative,
external basis, as in Jainism, but on a qualitative,
intentional basis. Just as the deed which produces
karma is not merely physical in nature, so, also,
the consequences of the deed are moral and spiritual as well as natural.[9] Ever since the *Bhagavad
Gita*, the dispositional sides of Hindu ethics have

[9] Cf. Sir Sivaswamy Aiyer: *Evolution of Hindu Moral Ideals.*

[183]

played a large role. When a correct intuitive relation with the superkarmic order is achieved, moreover, the change is absolute so that man's deepest being is free, even though the karmic forces still remaining must be used up, until death breaks the final bonds. If now, this relation with the superkarmic order can affect a person in this life, if the order of karma can be both modified and broken within the flux of the phenomenal world, God's redemptive relation to man can also become effective within the whole order of history and nature.

Since Hinduism has theistic sects, since its concept of ultimate reality as *saccidananda*, existence plus intelligence plus bliss, contains strong personal elements, and since Christianity itself must be careful not to limit God too much by the measure of men, the idea of personality in God need form no strong hindrance for the mutual understanding of Christianity and Hinduism. Hinduism needs, however, the idea of a redemptive Love, of a Purpose directly concerned with human affairs that loves, cares, and is able to save. This would inspire confidence in the masses.

This would lead Hinduism from a description of actuality to an affirmation of the ideal that can change *that* actuality. Since the inner motive conditions the production of karma, this redemptive idea seems consistent with Hinduism. Faith in such a God could produce the attitude necessary to overcome the production of enslaving karma; for detachment could become, as in the *Gita*, detachment not from action but in action, and the idea of detachment could then be clarified and developed to mean the attachment to a deeper reality beyond history, productive of an attachment to men in history which is not enslaving because it is itself bound to a deeper reality. Man would thus by faith in God be not only the victor over karma but the master of it, turning its forces positively to the salvation of history rather than yielding to belief in its necessarily enslaving nature. Karma itself can be redeemed, and will be when Indian pessimism is touched by Christian hope. God's forgiveness enters when through faith in God's grace man rises above the discouraging observations connected with karma to know that in spite of his sins and failures there is hope, not of escape from life but of victory over it. If the consequences of man's deeds are not eternal and if his intentions affect his deeds, then, indeed, we can agree with Radhakrishnan that: "We can insist with unflinching rigour on the inexorability of the moral law and yet believe in the forgiveness of sin."[10]

Since Hinduism stresses that intentions affect consequences, it provides ample room for social solidarity. Life is necessarily social. Our attitudes affect others. All living is through those who live and have lived. Sin and grace travel by the same channels. Man is continuously influenced in his attitudes by his social environment. Society profits by the past sufferings of its members, and through the present. It is helped by those who love and hope. Insofar as Hinduism is a fellowship of suffering seeking salvation, it ought to be able to understand how God's coming into the world to suffer for it, and His continuous suffering with it to save it unto a creative fellowship of joy, can and eventually must change the whole course of human history. If it were not for the

[10] Radhakrishnan: *The Hindu View of Life*, p. 74.

initiative of God's love and His redemptive activity in history, man could not be saved; but when man grasps through faith the source and strength of his salvation, his whole attitude changes and along with it the consequences which flow from it. When he thus acts as a member of the Kingdom of God, he affects the world he touches, and he becomes, as Luther put it, a savior to others. In its doctrine of *dharma*, or social duties, Hinduism already has a social doctrine. When it realizes that *dharma* is more than a result from the past, more than a present arrangement, and when it applies the notion of *dharma* to karma, then the eyes of Hinduism may be opened to the social and vicarious aspects of the deeper spiritual life.

This brings up a crucial issue. Does God's active work in history involve interference with the natural order? If human beings enjoy a measure of real freedom within the natural order, if human purposes can initiate chains of causation that will have their appropriate consequences, why cannot God's purpose be a larger, better, and more effective purpose? With every right

Dewick argues from the analogy of human activity that there is nothing unreasonable in God's effective working in the natural order.[11] The purpose of God does not deny the order of karma but works in and through it. If the world, as Ramanuja taught, is the body of God, His intentions would be reflected in His concrete deeds. This is especially easy to affirm in Hinduism since its view of the deepest reality is not materialistic but through and through spiritualistic. Up to this point we have reached, to be sure, only a Whiteheadian concept of God as the best and permanent purpose in process, but can we not go further and claim that these karmic forces have been created by God and are subservient to His will? God can then operate through them while still granting them a temporarily purposed independence. God works both indirectly through the laws of karma and directly within them. Naturally, this question is one of ultimates. Since Hinduism affirms, however, that the supra-karmic realm is the ultimately real, why cannot this realm be the Christian God? Karma is in

[11] Dewick: *The Indwelling God*, pp. 273-275.

that case on the plane no longer of illusion, but of a history open to God's redemptive action and to man's hope rather than despair. Man's freedom in the present is then the freedom of grace through faith to transform his life and history by the aid of a redemptive Will greater than the world.

Christianity, similarly, can learn much from Hinduism. Hinduism's distaste for Christianity's doctrine of a last minute forgiveness before death reveals especially Protestantism's rather superficial theology at this point. The Roman Catholic theologians, to be sure, have worked out the relation of sin and consequence with greater insight and care. In absolution only the guilt, not the consequences of the guilt, is pardoned. Forgiveness is thus kept on a personal, spiritual plane, while the order of nature is also respected. Penance and purgatory are doctrines which attempt to safeguard the natural order of things while still keeping forgiveness subject to immediate personal restoration. If a choice must be made between the natural and the spiritual order, we must, of course, take the latter: Christian forgiveness instead of Hindu karma, grace rather than merit; but such a choice is unnecessary. To make it is to become theologically inadequate. There is ample room and need for the theory of karma as the doctrine of deed and consequence within the larger order of God's grace.

Christian theology can learn from the Hindu idea of karma, however, only if it refuse to accept not only the idea that the consequences of man's deeds go on forever, but also the idea that upon God's forgiveness the consequences of sin are immediately abolished. By the former notion we arrive at an unwarranted naturalism; by the latter, at an unnecessary lawlessness. Both extremes are obviously untrue to experience. Instead, an adequate doctrine must recognize first of all that full forgiveness is on the personal plane, immediately redemptive, irrespective of consequences. The personal level is the deepest reality and operates according to spiritual laws, regardless of the direct or indirect consequences. There is also a natural plane where the consequences go on, but not forever. Nature tends to neutrality according to different rhythms, varying to a great degree in proportion to their relation to personal purpose. Hinduism has itself pondered just this question of the neutralizing of the consequences of good and evil deeds.[12] Marks in the rocks are erased but slowly, while wounds in the body heal much more quickly. In proportion as nature is alive it tends the more quickly to neutrality. Nature is like a dough of different consistencies with a constant tendency to regain its natural shape. If the personal and the natural levels are kept in mind, it is clear that a distinction must be made between them in Christian theology. In social life, though the relatives of a murdered man may forgive the murderer, he is hanged nevertheless. Although the wife who has been sinned against physically may forgive her husband, both may pay for the sin in their future family life. Even when God forgives such a sin, the natural penalty must be paid. God forgives, but the consequences in society and history go on—for a time. Since not endless cause and effect but restorative growth and creative activity characterize nature, the effects of sin go on, depending upon their nature, until they have be-

[12] Aiyer: *op. cit.*, p. 145.

come neutralized in the great receptacle of natural life.

The organic, reciprocal relation between the spiritual and the natural level must also be carefully observed. The personal affects the natural, and the natural the personal. If the soul is healed through forgiveness, the body is also the more quickly restored. That is why Jesus often began his healing by saying: "Thy sins are forgiven thee." "Fear not" is good medicine for both mind and body. The great advances in endocrinology indicate how emotional disturbances poison the blood. Freud well served his generation by pointing out the psychogenetic origin of much illness. Frequently hysteria is due to a sin-sick soul. To understand how the forgiveness of sin and confident faith in God can heal the body, the psychogenetic aspect of personal and social evil ought to be kept in mind. When restoration is made on the spiritual level of life, the restorative rhythm on the natural level is quickened. The natural order also affects the spiritual. "The spirit is willing but the flesh is weak." The body is the meeting place of personal purpose and natural chains of causation, and the traffic is not one way. When the natural order is not changed, influences from it may help to defeat the effects of forgiveness. Nature may overburden the spirit; karma may become man's dreaded yoke. The Roman Catholic demand is that the penitent avoid the same situation which caused him to sin. Those who have worked in rescue missions, or who have carefully studied their own lives, know how important it is to understand this relation between nature and spirit. Man's natural, economic, or social creations may exert such a pressure on his highest ideals as to dull or overcome his spirit. But if sin can work through nature, so can grace. Through man's means God can affect man's spirit. Through natural and historical ways the goodness of God can work to redeem man, bring him to Himself, make him feel the need for personal forgiveness and fellowship.

Even these brief comments indicate how the patient study of Hinduism may help us in thinking through some of our own theological problems. We preach theoretically that God has revealed Himself at all times and in all places.

Surely, we need all the light we can get. We speak about sharing with other faiths, but such sharing must be a thorough searching of consciences and doctrines. Can we relate our final faith in Christ to whatever new knowledge or problems are ours? Upon the satisfactory solution of the deep questions of theology reposes much of our effectiveness in relation to a religion like Hinduism. For that matter, as a recent article in the *Chinese Recorder* rightly stressed, it is important that we be able to hold the searching thinkers within our own Christian fold. Only the spirit of positive faith in the universality of Christ and in the intellectual tenability of his Gospel can bring in the new day. The way to religious victory is through a deeper understanding of the complete range of religious needs and religious insights.

VIII

The Christian Fellowship as a Social Theory

ONE of the major problems confronting the Christian fellowship is the social issue. In a rapidly changing world this question is becoming more and more critical. Is the Christian fellowship an adequate social theory? This problem ought to be faced frankly. Perhaps the fairest way to approach the issue is to compare the basic motif of the Christian fellowship with the basic motifs of the most important rival interpretations of our day.

The answers that we receive from life depend, of course, a great deal upon the questions that we ask of it. During certain periods of history, or within certain groups which possess definite, authoritative beliefs, the answers are always in terms of predetermined principles of interpretation. In this case the mind can be free to speculate without ultimate confusion since it has some standards of truth which can direct its gropings by providing fixed ultimates. But history also shows us periods of bewilderment; and even within every ideological group there are some who question the very foundations of faith, who doubt the validity of the way it asks its fundamental questions. To-day we are experiencing a period of unusual confusion, inasmuch as both outside and inside every great faith there is a serious reexamination of the basis of belief. Especially obvious is this confusion among those liberals who have no allegiance to any ultimate standard of interpretation, be it social, political, or religious. These liberals are usually lacking in consistency of long range purpose, and are almost invariably nervous concerning present problems because of a lack of absolute focus from which to view contemporary developments.

Very few scholars can be experts in any fundamental approach to life; and rare are those who can master more than one. And yet our training and even our daily reading and thinking are buffeted and torn among several world views based on widely diverging assumptions. The man who is an expert in none may be aware in his own mind of a continual conflict among a number of points of view. The battle-field, indeed, lies deeper than his mind, far down in the recesses of his past training and emotional conditioning; and often before he is even conscious of a preliminary skirmish, the combat is upon him with full force. At times, however, there is not even a battle, but there springs unexpectedly from ambush a flash of thought or a wave of feeling which is perplexingly incongruous to the way he was previously thinking or feeling. In the midst of a sermon or even a prayer, for example, a thought may slip into his mind which he recognizes has no place in the Christian way of looking at things. Or again, when he is mentally relaxed and receptive, several conflicting motifs like so many exploding bomb-shells may flash successively before him. On analysis it seems that there are to-day particularly four ways of looking at life and of asking it questions, which, if not engaged in open combat, at least carry on a kind of guerrilla warfare. These four are the ways of Fascism, Communism, Freudianism, and Christianity.

When, for instance, we ponder the truth of

the reported saying of Jesus that "Whosoever hath, to him shall be given, and he shall have abundance: but whosoever hath not, from him shall be taken even that which he hath," the notion strikes us with force that this statement is really more in the spirit of Fascism than in the spirit of Christianity. How strangely, for instance, it contrasts with the motif underlying the parable of the laborers in the vineyard who received equal reward for unequal labor. The very fact that Christianity could contain a sentiment like "to him that hath" has held back more than one from professing to be a Christian. When, on the other hand, gripped by a novel or a play on the theme that true wealth consists not in worldly possessions but in spiritual resources, we may feel deeply stirred and even rejoice in the thought that true riches may not be denied us as worldly riches have been, until a sudden, rebellious thought wells up: You fool! You are falling prey to Capitalistic propaganda. All we have absorbed from the reading of Communistic literature insinuates that Christianity supports Capitalism; for it is the other-worldliness of Christianity, its stress on the inner life, which makes it possible for owners of almost uncountable wealth to suppress a more and more enlightened mass of workers. Then again, in the midst of our struggle to reach an explanation of a phase of the problem of evil, why the wicked flourish while the saints suffer, a disturbing thought leaps up to confound us: the wicked may not really be wicked; they are perhaps only better adjusted than the saints. Why should not the saints with all their suppressions suffer? Perhaps the very fact that they are saints bespeaks the truth that there is in their lives something against which they must struggle harder than most people. What happened in their childhood to make them fit so ill with the world? A peculiarly self-sacrificing person may elicit emotions first of admiration, then of contempt as it occurs to us that his seemingly unselfish service may spring from no other ultimate motive than to be thought well of, and finally of pity, as we realize that he is not responsible for this condition if he is only a football kicked back and forth by his deeper unknown self and his unnatural environment. Then we wake up with a shock to the knowledge that instead of dealing with the problem of evil from the Christian point of view, we have been almost completely engrossed in the Freudian approach. So life goes on, with basic motifs in restless conflict. It is well worth our while, therefore, to think through those four fundamental ways of looking at life that so hauntingly challenge the validity of our every assertion.

One meaningful approach to the understanding of Fascism is through the ideas of Vilfredo Pareto, whose pre-Fascist writings seem at many points to tally remarkably with what is actually going on in Fascist states. He proposes that every form of society is almost entirely biologically determined. Man's thoughts and acts are mostly the expression of his passional reason and can change only negligibly his social situation. Society in the aggregate has a certain unchangeable structure because it is biologically determined. Through all history the proportion of the rich to the poor, the strong to the weak, the ruling to the governed has been essentially the same. By his lengthy investigations Pareto aimed to prove the applicability of the law of mathematical equilibrium to socio-economics. The social balance between classes remains the same, but not the people in it. Those who control the power of any given society change in various rhythms in accordance with their ability to remain hardhearted. Those who are powerful must be ruthless; they must pursue their goal without scruple. Those who can and dare to take the power are the élite. Since, however, these possessors of power tend to regain their scruples with the cessation of upward struggle, tend to become thwarted through sympathy and to decay through the irrational morbidity of religious emotions, they must eventually give way to those who are more determined to have the power. This process of disintegration is always going on within the ruling class, so that the élite are said to circulate, according to a law governing society as a whole which leaves the class relations as such invariably the same.

The world is thus ruled not by the meek but by the strong; not by right, but by might. Civilizations rise and decay, systems of ethics and re-

ligion are born and die; but those who have the
will to power and dare to use it, they and they
alone rule the world. Those crushed beneath the
heel of the strong then rationalize their situation
and formulate for themselves slave moralities to
obtain whatever happiness can be theirs. On and
on go the cycles, the rich become the poor, the
weak become the strong; Feudalism, Capitalism,
Communism, Fascism: whatever be the content
held by the flux of social change, the form itself
remains immutable; the law of might remains
unchanged.

These ideas are easily applied to nations. The
nations which know what they want and will
not hesitate to use whatever methods are needed
to get it will dominate those nations which have
decayed into that soft sentimentalism which they
euphemistically call international morality. Particularly, too, can this principle be applied to
races. The Nordics are of a race which worships
courage, whereas certain other races have become enslaved by the weakening sentimentalism
and guile which is called universal morality, the
purpose of which is the protection of the weak

who dare not break it. That nation and race, therefore, which dares to take and wield relentless power is the one which history must call supreme. To develop sympathy for other nations or races is the greatest of all dangers. Within the nation the weaklings must be dominated or exterminated, lest the nation itself become a nation of weaklings. Outside the nation, the weaker nations must be subjugated, possessed as quickly as possible, while only those nations can be dealt with on any basis of equality which know themselves to be strong, which tolerate no vitiating, enfeebling sentimentalism, which dare to oppose strength with strength. The strong must stand together to possess the weak. This is the transvaluation of all values of which Nietzsche wrote. It is the final revolt against the slave morality of Christianity. It is the only world view which works, which history has itself proved to be right. The stress on the strong nation or race can supplant the stress on the group, the State which is the Party led and symbolized by a particularly strong man can become the nation which has no will, wish, or thought outside the State, as described in the writings of Giovanni Gentile, and loyalty to the State can become more important than the individual's push to power. So can Pareto's principle be extended until it becomes all-important in relation to the nation and the race. His theory of the inevitable rule of power grounded in biological determinism marches on; rapidly it begins to girdle the world.

Pareto's ideas are particularly haunting because of their basis on fact. His interpretation reflects not a little ugly actuality. He could not attribute changes in society to economic factors as ultimate principles of interpretation since he rightly observed that mere having does not assure continuance of power. Being he found in the long run to be a more fundamental category than having. Those who are strong will get the power; they will take it. In every kind of social organization the strong have found a way to push ahead and push those who weaken to the wall. The idea that America, for example, no longer offers opportunities for the poor to rise is absurd in view of the verdict of history. The pace may change, but not the process. The strong

have always eventually reached the top, and
might has seemed to determine the right. Within
the classes there has always been change, but the
classes themselves have remained. This idea seems
equally applicable to the relation of nations to
each other. Why is Hitler going through with
a program of political expansion which may
eventuate in his realizing more than the dreams
of old Germany and Austria combined? Will he
some day dominate the European Continent and
control the Dardanelles? Why cannot Mussolini
control Spain and the Mediterranean and then
start a drive alongside that of Germany, flanking
the Berlin-Bagdad line, and thus control Britain's
whole immediate access to the Far East, which is
itself being wrested from the democracies by another Power unashamed? Was it because the
democracies had become demoralized by a sentimental idealism? Even as long ago as during the
first year of the Spanish war, many a thinker
forefelt the inevitable: the eventual back-down
of the democracies. It seemed inevitable due to
the popular feeling about war, the fear of Communism on the part of the rich, and the sick

consciences of the leaders of democracy from much reading about the evils of a dictated peace. With sinking hearts we watched the sending of a British Commission to Prague and Chamberlain's flight to Munich, and feared with good reason that the theatrics alone remained.[1]

Pareto's views are based on actuality so much as to be no less haunting than the clichés: "There always will be wars," and "You can't change human nature." He denies the basic affirmations of Christianity and Communism alike, for while Christianity asserts that you can change the world by the changing of human nature, Communism insists that you can change the world by the changing of the economic order. Here he is more akin to Freudianism in agreeing that civilization is explainable in biological terms, although his diagnosis and suggested treatment are far different from those of Freud.

Pareto observed history and concluded that the order of the world as a whole was fixed. Karl Marx, on the other hand, looked at the

[1] This chapter was written shortly before the outbreak of the European war!

world to discover the root of its evil in order to eliminate it. Pareto accepted the actual world; Marx tried to interpret it in order to change it. The basic answer to life's problems he proposed to be economic. As he looked on life to determine what made the wheels of civilization go around, he saw that mankind's history as a whole, man's endeavors, man's will to power, man's desire for recognition, man's actual control of situations— all of man's activities were somehow bound up with material wealth. Not that every individual man was completely and directly determined by his economic condition, but that every civilization as a whole was different according to the way the forces that could produce wealth were owned and employed. The whole structure of society ultimately expressed, he observed, the control and use of the means of production. Every group in it responded differently to each type of society in proportion to its being benefited or harmed by it. However expressed, the struggle was invariably between control and oppression, between having and not having.

All social questions, consequently, could ultimately be answered in economic terms. The literature produced in a given society would as a whole be that defending the *status quo*. The literary output of the oppressed in the Capitalist State would tend to be branded as subversive and, if possible, banned out of existence. The best literary forms to protect society would naturally be the indirect and symbolic. Moral and religious writers, preachers, and teachers would be especially valuable to make the masses think that morality is founded on absolute, immutable supernatural ideals, or even better, in the watchful will of a living God. Morality and religion could thus be invoked to cow the masses, and to allay their material desires by focussing them on the inner riches of the spirit or the inestimable treasures of a future life. The poor like to sing: "I walk with the King, Hallelujah," "My Father is rich in silver and gold," and "There'll be no disappointment in heaven." All literature, moreover, could be used to make live imaginatively what was denied in reality. Even history became interpreted to prove that those who actually deserved it, by accepting things as they were, would in the long run be owners of wealth. The Capitalists could do this because they knew that even though the workers might spend their evenings denouncing the rich, their fondest hope would always be to become one of them.

Marx observed this and felt that there could be no permanent solution of the problems of life until man was freed from the love of having. He agreed with the Bible that "the love of money is the root of all evil," and felt that man was so constituted that mankind as a whole could never find the perfect society until all wealth was commonly owned, until that which separates men and makes them do things that they would not do unless they were the servants of Mammon could be used for the common good of all, to cement rather than to rend men asunder. But who was to effect this beautiful dream of a new earth where dwelt peace and righteousness? The workers who had nothing, who had not been spoilt by the love of possession: they should be taught the ideal world, taught that their greatest good was not to become rich here or in heaven, but to dwell in a classless society where wealth

would be produced according to each one's ability and be used according to each one's needs.
This could naturally be accomplished only by a
revolution, since the rich would always be too
blinded by the riches of this world to desire any
radical and permanent change. Class consciousness on the part of the proletariat was only a
means to classlessness, to individual freedom. For
a while, therefore, the workers would have for-
cibly to suppress those vitiated by the old order
of things until the Community of the Classless
could be established, when the forceful defense
of the common good would give way to spontaneous fellowship, free creativity, and an economy of abundance.

The power that Communism actually holds
over its adherents, the martyrdom which many
are ready to endure for it, the continual sacrifices
which its members offer—these cannot be explained without recognizing the basis for Communism as somehow vitally grounded both in
fact and in ideal. Not to recognize Karl Marx as
one of the prophets is to fail of his vision. He
revived and universalized the old Jewish dream

of a perfect society on earth. The basic motifs of Marxism are much more akin to Christianity than to Fascism or to Freudianism. If, therefore, we are to take issue with Karl Marx in the name of Christianity, we must do so with our eyes open to what he really saw and wished to accomplish. For that reason, to say that Communism stands for the class struggle except as a necessary but temporary expedient is entirely to misunderstand it; for Communism stands wholly and determinedly, according to the ideas of Marx, for the final establishment of the classless society, where there is neither oppressor nor oppressed, but only a great brotherhood of joint creators living amicably together.

A third approach to life is offered by Freudianism. In the light of its basic principle of interpretation, our deepest problems are seen as unconscious in nature, consciousness hiding from us the ugly facts that we wish not to see. These disturbances of the unconscious are sexual in nature, since sex, far more than a localized function, is, indeed, the basic drive of life. Our deeper self has certain psychic energies to discharge in ways natural to it, but is prevented from doing so by the conscious, socialized self, the ego, which is struggling with the unnaturalness of society as represented within each self by the parental self, the superego. Whatever social and individual maladjustment there is, is due to the fact that our lives are prevented from being natural by a society which is itself ultimately the product of a necessary sexual inhibition and therefore of a sexual unnaturalness which causes tensions and displacements, and which perpetuates this unnaturalness through the parental image in the child by means of an authoritative conscience and a destructive sense of guilt. Our real difficulties therefore, are with a society which is itself so ill adjusted to the basic drive of life that it almost automatically produces problems of infantile sexuality, causes us to harbor undischarged psychical energy, supports repressions from which we try to escape by symptoms such as mental or physical illnesses or by sublimations such as religious illusions, a sense of security through possessions, or social approval through position. All social activities are secondary to the sexual drive, the

creativity of life itself. Every sphere of man's
endeavors can, and the Freudians hope, will, be
explained in the light discovered by psycho-
analysis. Religion is an illusion, an unconsciously
motivated attempt to avoid the individual's maladjustment to society by regression, the wishful
return to the heavenly harmony of the mother's
womb; or projection, the wishful creation of a
dream world; or compensation, the obtaining of
social substitutes for the deeper desires of the
natural man.

Freud was both an unusually productive scientist and a Jewish prophet. His sincere desire, no
doubt, was to know the truth that it might make
us free. With his diagnosis of individual and
social maladies, he suggests as a cure, therefore,
the discovery of the causes by a return to the
original repression, by the tracing back to the
conflicts in early childhood where the discharge
of the psychic energy of infantile sexuality
stopped. The conscious man, however, having
been taught that the things he suffers from are
wrong, has no access to the unconscious source
of his trouble. A trained psychiatrist, on the

other hand, through the patient's continued disclosure of his past, and particularly of his dreams, can by this method of free association construct a pattern through which he can, so to speak, trick from the unconscious its destructive secret. For a cure to be permanently effective, the original source must invariably be discovered. Thus Freud could say to us in our sufferings that except we become as little children we shall in no wise enter the Kingdom of Nature. After the discovery and frank recognition of the basic cause, the individual self must learn to resume its natural growth, to face a world of reality instead of a world of phantasy, to break out of its isolation and discard substitutes for real fellowship, to live a natural life through whatever forms of society provide the most successful sublimations. The chief social aspect of Freud's way to a better world was that most of the burden of responsibility for society lies with the parents, who must themselves be freed from their unnatural living in order not to transmit it to their children by example; must be informed as to the destructive influence certain teachings would have on society to come; and must rear their children in the enlightenment provided by psychoanalytic truth. In order to appraise Freudianism, along with Fascism and Communism, in the light of our native Christianity, we must now restate concisely the meaning of Christianity itself.

Our understanding of the Christian fellowship as a social theory is in terms of the basic teachings of Jesus and of the Christian Church. When we are told that there was nothing distinctive in the teachings of Jesus, we are considerably perplexed to explain the way in which Christianity swept the world in spite of the advanced philosophies of the ancient world. It had to face rivals of a high caliber, first Judaism, Stoicism, and Greek syncretism, to mention but a few; then Neo-Platonism and Mithraism. Some great idea seems to have propelled the rapid rise of Christianity against heavy odds. The three ideas, God, duty, and immortality, which Harnack makes the essentials of Christianity, were already part and parcel of both Greek and Jewish thought. The Fatherhood of God and the Brotherhood of man were common teachings among the Stoics, albeit in terms of divine immanence, and were at least potentially present in the daily sayings of the Jewish faith: "Thou shalt love the Lord thy God" and "thy neighbor as thyself." The historic person of Jesus by itself cannot explain Christianity, for only by means of the permanent principles with which they identify themselves are men lastingly great. Much is said about the Golden Rule being the distinctive teaching of Jesus; but although this is to some extent true, we find almost the same sentiment in Jewish apocryphal literature, in Confucius' and Mencius' doctrine of *jen*, or reciprocal benevolence, in Stoicism's stress on the natural brotherhood of man. Jesus' view of life goes far beyond that of the Golden Rule.

In order to make comparison possible, it is necessary to review the basic teachings of Christianity. Jesus developed in concrete cases and in incidental teachings the full implications of the meaning of love as the chief characteristic of God and as the supreme duty of man. He also combined, whatever be the explanation in terms of source or original creativity, the Jewish idea of a personal God not only above the world, but working in it toward a definite goal, with Stoic universalism. This love, furthermore, was not only reciprocal, but redemptive. Jesus taught a Kingdom of God, of which he himself seems to have claimed to be, in some sense, the Messiah, where God's will for perfect love, purity, and humility would everywhere be done, where there would be full freedom and faithfulness in fellowship. Those who lost themselves in this fellowship would thereby find life more abundantly. Jesus himself now lived in the Kingdom, and those who would be his disciples must live there too; they must turn the other cheek and forgive seventy times seven; they must not refuse those who wish to borrow from them, nor even withhold their garments; they must be perfect even as their heavenly Father. Jesus taught the ideal life of the Kingdom which he expected immediately, not the practical life of this world; councils of heavenly perfection, not practical precepts for the ways of the world. The children of the Kingdom must practice positive, unlimited good will, even when this means a cross unto persecution and death.

After Jesus' death, the disciples became con-

[217]

vinced that God had acted through Jesus' suffering to redeem man and make him divine. Underlying all narrowing theological superstructures
and historical limitations, even seemingly in the
minds of the disciples, is this basic idea of God's
redemptive love. The way to a new heaven and
a new earth was by the positive preaching and
practicing of the Gospel of Good Will, to use
President William Dewitt Hyde's phrase, a good
will rooted in God Himself. The early Christians
did not, however, believe in the gradual growth
of a God-given good will, but were so confident
that Jesus would soon return that they sold all
they had and spent their days living communis-
tically, waiting for him in the Temple. At first,
for a century and a half, according to Cadoux,
they practiced an ethics of world renunciation,
refusing to bear arms. They then changed, as
they grew in numbers, first to an ethics of world
transcendence, an intermediary stage workable
as long as they were a suppressed minority; but
when Christianity became the State religion, as
the Church became the world, the problem
changed almost completely, and Christianity ac-

cepted an ethics of world affirmation. What else could it do? When all Romans were Christians, could they do nothing to defend civilization against the Huns, against the Barbarians, against the Mohammedans? Long before this, of course, Christians had joined the army, but now the whole army fought with the explicit sanction of the Church. It became the Christian doctrine, therefore, that every action must be motivated by complete good will and applied in whatever way is practically best in the actual world.

Those who would say that this ethics of world affirmation is contrary to the teachings of Jesus forget that his expectation that God would bring in His Kingdom almost immediately led him to leave principles of perfection, not practical instructions. A small minority could practice world renunciation, but this attitude would do little directly to settle actual problems. Then, too, the God whom the Christians called omnipotent and holy love had made this kind of world and was supposed to work in this actual world not only by persuasion, but by physically punishing His people even through heathen hands in order finally to save them. If God could do this, why not His children? In spite of the anthropomorphism of the idea, the problem as to God's relation to the actual world will not down. In a world like this, love must operate through judgment as well as through persuasion. Force cannot be avoided. The real question is if it can be motivated by good will and directed by an adequate reasonableness. War is Christian only when it is motivated by rationally directed good will toward the people *against* whom it is waged. Unless we are to surrender our Christian conception of love as by its very nature unlimited, we must accept as Christian a God-centered ethics of world affirmation on the part of the Church.[2] This leaves us with an understanding of Christianity as God's Gospel of Good Will, as both means and end, as both inclusive of love's persuasion and rationally directed force, as both the way and the reality of the Kingdom of God. It is this view of Christianity with which we must confront the "isms."

[2] After a year of struggling with the problem, the author still feels that Christian ethics must be genuinely world affirming, but that Christian world affirmation must always be subordinate to a world transcendence which at times makes world renunciation painfully necessary.

The basic motif of Fascism is that social biology must be recognized as life's deepest principle of interpretation, wherein for both the strong and the weak might is right. Against this Christianity pitches its faith in the ultimacy of a free and responsible community grounded in God, through Whom every member is an end with his own inalienable worth. Christianity holds that the ideal is ultimately more true than the actual, with power enough to change it. The only way in which the two can be compared is in terms of their respective ideals and the judgment of history. As to ideals, Professor Ralph Barton Perry points out that values can be compared only in three ways: according to intensity, preference, and inclusiveness. The first two are personal and highly variable in nature. The third has possibilities for descriptive comparison. From this point of view the Christian ideal is the higher, for it includes all people. The satisfaction of a few is not based on the suppression of the many. The preference of a few or the intensity of their experience are judgments incapable of becoming general and inclusively satisfactory social laws. The question is not of a minority judgment innately better than the general opinion, not of a defense of the *status quo*, but of an ideal capable of being the highest possible social ideal. Kant believed that this notion of every individual's being an end, not a means, could be rationally proved from the nature of the moral law; but even if we should grant that this specific content could not spring out of an empty form, nevertheless, even on a descriptive, pragmatic level alone, the Christian ideal seems unquestionably the higher; for even though Fascism speaks of true freedom as bestowed on the individual by the State, the mass of individuals have actually little freedom of their own, and are, even in theory, means living solely for the State.

In the actual world, moreover, there are forms of government closer to the Christian ideal than Fascism. Christianity is not necessarily Democracy in the sense of majority rule, but Democracy is both ideally and actually closer to Christianity than is Fascism. Given a world with talents of far different orders, a sincere and intelligent paternalism may temporarily be a better form of government than complete democracy,

[222]

if this were immediately attainable; but Democracy seems theoretically most consistent with the ultimate and deeper equality of God's children.

As for the actual world, as we saw in Chapter II, we can discern in the history of the ages a gradual increase in the value of the individual. This could be illustrated in a thousand ways: the way in which history has moved from the exposure of infants to the incubation of premature babies; from the killing of the old and decrepit to the fight to preserve them and make them comfortable by every means of modern medicine; from male dominance in family life to the democratic modern marriage based on freedom rather than on economic bondage; from the early cosmogonies in philosophy to "the subjectivist bias" and existential philosophy. The freedom of the individual became in recent times stressed even to the point where a collectivistic reaction was needful. In a Christian world, both freedom and fellowship must be given full emphasis. The historical development, too, has progressed from family to tribal modes of social organization, and then gradually into larger and larger modes of togetherness. We have come even to the place where not only economically, but in every phase of history, nationalism in terms of tense hatred or uncontrolled will to have one's own way is beginning to be outmoded. Even national sovereignty as a notion must soon yield to national loyalty, deep enough to cooperate with other nations like men, too deep to fly into a childish tantrum unless one unquestionably gets his way. Thus, on grounds both of actuality and of ideal, it is a convincing fact that Christianity is a better way of looking at life, and that the long-run view of history supports it against the Fascist attempt to stop the clock-hand of history.

The deepest thought in Communism is probably that man's troubles have an economic root, so that if the temptation to selfishness in this respect were removed, society would be free to live in the deeper fellowship where the good of each would be the good of all, and the good of all the good of each. Collectivism in the sense of totalitarian compulsion was considered by Marx merely a temporary means to the individual good, or to freedom in fellowship. One can hardly help agreeing with Marx that Capitalism has solved the problem of production but not that of distribution, that there is an incongruity in the co-existence of overproduction and general need, and that the ideal is the society where man is not separated by conditions which make for selfishness. One can hardly sit under the Kremlin walls without pondering the Communistic stress on being and doing rather than mere having. And yet to be a Communist is impossible while the Christian way seems to be truer. St. Augustine said that Neo-Platonism had the right philosophy, but did not know the way to realize it. So Communism has a fundamental insight, but does not see the way to make it real. We cannot free men from bondage to things by the mere abolishing of classes. The trouble goes deeper than social organization. It may not, in general, be fair to argue from the history of Russia so far, but one thing stands out unmistakably, that the cleft between the rulers and the ruled is still there. Psychologically those in power feel themselves and are felt to be distinct. The rewards and privileges, also, are in general distributed in accordance with the individual's power and value to society. It is amazing to learn of the differences in reward even within the same factories. Christianity would, of course, be unwise not to recognize that social organization has effect on character and that it must strive not only to change individual lives, but to attain whatever form of social organization, educational, economic, political, best fits freedom and faithfulness in fellowship. It would be still more unwise, however, if it believed that it could change the world merely by the changing of the external modes of social organization. Although extensive changes are important, far more important is the intensive growth of good will without which no desirable form of society is feasible. Bergson rightly maintains that only religious creativity can break the limiting forms, the barriers, between men, that the world must be changed from the inside out. The economic evil is both oppressive and complex. The true prophet, while denouncing it, must stand perplexed before it; but there can be no cure until men are the masters of wealth, not its slaves. The way to mastery, moreover, is not by evading the temptation to destructive selfishness, but by developing the moral strength to overcome it. It seems, therefore, that Christianity is right in calling material goods the means for the development of character and the media of creative community. It is difficult to see how the class struggle, or even more, revolution, could develop an unlimited good will, or how man could be made good either through the absence of temptation or by the compulsion of the State. Since good will is a prerequisite of the good society, the mere removing of the economic temptation, the communizing of wealth, will not make for a human nature that can then dispense with the power of the State. Marxism is too naïve; its view of man and of his relation to nature is inadequate. To be realistic, we must remain Christian. Christianity is not confined to any mode of economic organization. It teaches that man can develop dignity, responsibility, and creativity in relation to private property without envy, pride, self-sufficiency, or bitterness, but that man's moral development lags far behind his technological progress. Christianity thus denies both the

[227]

thesis of Fascism, that human nature cannot be changed, and that of Communism, that it can be changed by the simple solution of changing the external order of things.

The fundamental idea of Freudianism seems to be that the troubles of the world are rooted in the unconscious depths of human psyches. The ills of the world must be cured by having the sufferers recognize the nature of their malady, turn from a world of phantasy to the world of reality, and have their displacements redirected into socially valuable channels. Although it claims itself to be naturalistic and deterministic, Freudianism has most interesting material for Christian interpretation. The fact that illnesses seemed to be strictly physiological in the sense that laws of nature are unchangeable by the laws of mind, or the idea that the brain and glands accounted for the conditions of life: these ideas might mean that consciousness itself was the product of the brain, that what we call the soul was nothing but a physical effect. William James claimed that the brain transmitted consciousness, and this thought became more than crumbs for those who willed to believe; but now come Freud and the Freud-

ians telling us that the psyche as a whole is what
accounts for bodily conditions. No matter if it
is called naturalistic, no matter if the trouble is
called unconscious; as far as both the cause and
the cure are concerned, they are conscious in
nature, according to the common use of that
term! Somehow there was something in the conscious world, the world of parents, social conditions, duty, natural urges, that the child through
wrong interpretation connected with shame and
guilt and did not want to face; and somehow the
patient, in order to be cured, must be made conscious of the nature of his sickness. Granted that
the cause was unconscious, the consciousness
must at least have been aware of it to suppress it
and keep it suppressed. Freud's own explanations
seem to hide the fact that both the ego and the
superego originate, however indirectly, in the
conscious world of human relationships and that
inhibitions are crowded with social references.
The Freudian view affirms the Christian teachings that the self is made for love, not loneliness.
Yes, Jesus' emphasis on faith, his healing, his con-
necting of physical healing with the forgiveness
of sin—the Freudian view stresses the deepest

Christian truths. But Freudianism, too, like Marxism, is too naïve. The cross is not only psychological, but cosmological; Jesus refused to connect the man's blindness with sin, either his own or his parents'. The suffering of the saints is not only because they are maladjusted, but because the world is sinful; and those who are best adjusted to the divine order must necessarily be out of joint with the evil in the world. The Cross of Jesus must still be borne, and in his spirit of self-forgetting love. By the strength of their inner lives and by the results of their lives, the saints prove that they are not pathological, but that the world is out of joint. If, moreover, people are so lonely that they are helped by believing in someone with the image of God in him, how much more are they helped by a firm faith in God Himself, and by an ideal of not worrying about what people think of them, but desiring in sincere humility to be of constant service. The psycho-genetic stress of Freudianism has only helped to strengthen and sustain a considered faith in the validity of the Christian approach to life.

Christianity, then, is the widest category that

we can find, for in it we can see the "isms" as partial truths: Fascism's insistence on the stubbornness of human nature and of social evil based on power, but its refusal to see the reality of the ideal in human history; Communism's dream of a new society relieved of the economic causes of evil, but its naïve belief in its impatient, contradictory short-cut to it; and Freudianism's emphasis on the psychogenesis of suffering, but without an adequate understanding of the conscious and ideal nature of the psyche. Not without foundation, therefore, do we continue to believe in and work for that fellowship which is grounded not only in sociological, economic, or even psychological categories, but, deeper yet, in Him whose complete freedom is also complete faithfulness.

Index

INDEX